BREAKING PROCRASTINATION BARRIERS - NAVIGATING STUDENT LIFE WITH PURPOSE

From Identifying Causes to Implementing Solutions - A Step-by-Step Guide for Students

SKY BENSON

BREAKING PROCRASTINATION BARRIERS - NAVIGATING STUDENT LIFE WITH PURPOSE

BY

(SKY BENSON)

This is a work of creative nonfiction. Some parts have been fictionalized in varying degrees for various purposes.

Sky Benson

Email: info@skysplace.com

Procrastination, lack of discipline, inertia, time management, and academic productivity are the sole topics covered in this book. Stop being a couch potato and start making progress!

Disclaimer

The purpose of this book is mainly to provide broad information. Despite having taken every precaution to guarantee the accuracy and completeness of the information provided, the Author disclaims all express and implied warranties and representations regarding the availability, suitability, accuracy, completeness, and reliability of the content found on these pages.

Nothing in this book should be used to replace knowledgeable financial, legal, or other expert advice. To obtain specific answers to their questions and concerns, readers are encouraged to consult with experts in the various disciplines discussed in this book.

The publisher and the author both disclaim any liability for any injury that results from using the advice in this book. All liability for any results arising from the use of any particular product, service, or organization referenced in this work is claimed by the Author and the Publisher.

The views expressed in this book are the Author's alone and do not represent the views of any organizations, individuals, or groups that are mentioned. The author of this book retains all rights to the text. Except for brief extracts from reviews or other noncommercial uses permitted by copyright law, no part of this publication may be reproduced, disseminated, or transmitted in any way without the express written permission of the author.

By using this book, you agree to the terms and conditions. Any issues that may occur because of heeding the recommendations in this book are not the responsibility of the author or the publisher.

TABLE OF CONTENTS

INTRODUCTION

At an extremely early age, human beings acquire the ability to use their minds. Our first day of school is between the ages of five and eight. At this point in our lives, we emerge from our shells to learn how the world operates and how we must physically and psychologically adjust to it. We were enrolled in school by our parents so that they could instruct us on how to live our lives. In the atmosphere that we are a part of at school, there is a wide range of personalities displayed by individuals. Things are taught to us by both the environment and the teachers that we have. Following that, we started to adjust to that environment. The latest information started to become available to us. We are expected to begin to work together. We start to spend an excessive amount of time in that environment, which is the school, learning new things and experiencing new things. This procedure has been ongoing for years now. Although we continue to get knowledge from that setting, regardless of whether we are in high school, college, or both, people will eventually stop exerting an excessive amount of work in order to keep their academic status as it is.

At the beginning of the school year, teachers start putting in a lot of effort to assist students in being more organized, ambitious, consistent, and punctual. However, around a specific age or following a particular experience, teenagers start to make their own choices regarding their lives. At that same time, neither the parents nor teachers can change their actions, efforts, way of thinking, or dreams for their lives. Children and teenagers start to procrastinate. They stop putting an excessive amount of effort into their academics. They will become lazy if they do not consider the implications of their activities in the present and how those acts may influence them in the future. Students frequently struggle with procrastination, which is one of the challenges they face throughout their academic careers. Students who engage in the practice of procrastination are those who engage in the act of putting off or delaying activities that are required to be accomplished. They start putting off important duties, which typically leads to frantic last-minute scrambling and increased levels of anxiety throughout the situation. For a variety of reasons, students could put off completing assignments. It can be brought on by a wide variety of factors, ranging from psychological concerns to environmental factors. Students in today's world commonly struggle with procrastination, and it is essential to conquer these challenges to keep one's motivation and concentration levels high. In a similar vein, it is of equal significance with regard to health.

Studying diligently can transform individuals and civilizations in ways that extend beyond the content of textbooks and the classroom. Making education a priority enables individuals to develop their intellectual capacities, take advantage of a wide range of opportunities, and contribute to the improvement of society. It is imperative that we focus on our objectives and make efforts to enhance our future since doing so will make it possible for us to accomplish our objectives and make progress in the future. It is not enough for a student to meet their deadlines to overcome procrastination. It is an approach that can be used for intellectual and personal development. The development of essential life skills, the establishment of a more balanced and healthier attitude toward their academic and professional commitments, and the laying of the groundwork for long-term success are all extremely important for students to accomplish. Whether they can manage their time, fight procrastination, and build a growth mentality will determine their future.

If you are here, it is safe to assume that you are not happy with some part of your life right now, most likely your tendency to procrastinate. If you are unhappy with the direction your life is taking professionally or, personally, or even both, this book can help you change your perspective and achieve more success in both areas. If students want to be successful in overcoming their procrastination, they must first determine the factors that contribute to it and then devise strategies to address those factors. The tactics for attaining your goals, maintaining your motivation, adopting an innovative attitude to life, and beginning to build a brighter future are the primary topics covered in this book. By the time you reach the conclusion of this book, you will have gained an understanding of the fundamentals of effective time management, future motivation, greater productivity, and self-discipline. You will be able to breeze through each day with ease and confidence if you put the principles that are covered in this book into practice. Reading this book will provide you with more knowledge about being a student, procrastination, and the ways in which it impacts your academic performance. You will also discover practical steps that you can take starting tomorrow to improve each of these areas of your life. Although the effectiveness of strategies to combat procrastination grows with repetition, it does not imply you cannot start right away!

CHAPTER 1

THE BEGINNINGS OF
PROCRASTINATION

I will tell you my story first, though. I was a brilliant child when I went to school, just like many other kids. I used to be a punctual person who put in the necessary effort to be a brilliant child. However, I eventually began to become sluggish. I became indolent, started shifting my priorities, and found it difficult to stick to my deadlines. I was cool in that setting at first, but one night, I considered what I was doing with my life. Even though I was being irresponsible, I was experiencing tension and anxiety from repeatedly failing. Is it still possible for me to have the future I desire despite my current situation? Can I Continue to Be Lazy and Postpone My Work and Still Be Successful? 'No', that was the answer. One can only enjoy the results of one's labors. Then it dawned on me that I could not risk my future. Then I came to know the term procrastination. After experiencing consistent failure for two years, I decided to make a permanent change in my behavior. To be completely open, I can now see that things are changing and that, yes, there is still hope for me to make amends and work on my future by being understanding when necessary. I still have time to modify my course of action. Additionally, having this perspective makes you more driven to take care of yourself, which is exactly what is occurring to me right now.

If you have decided to read this book, you could be familiar with procrastination, just like I am. It usually does not need an introduction, particularly if you have known it your entire life. Procrastination has been hovering in the background, pushing you to do what is worse for you as well, ever since you were old enough to realize that you actually have the option to have more fun rather than sit down to do your assignments. It is like a shadow because you cannot get rid of it. It is constantly there, and it is not simple to forget about. It is most determined to destroy your life.

Now that it is beginning to control you, you are stuck with it and experiencing issues, much like those relationships that were enjoyable at first but have now ruined practically every part of your life. You want to end this toxic relationship to put your life back on track, but you are not sure how to do it. The key, though, lies in understanding how to reclaim control over procrastination's depressing influence ultimately. To start changing your ways, you must first understand what this leech is in reality. It begins with gaining a true understanding of procrastination and the various guises it assumes when attempting to manipulate you into giving it control once more.

What is procrastination in literal meaning?

Before getting solutions, it is crucial first to understand what is meant by the term "procrastination." Crastinus means "of tomorrow," while pro means "forward, forth, or in favor of." These two Latin terms are the source of the English word "procrastination." Thus, it might literally mean delaying anything till tomorrow or thinking that tomorrow is the greatest time to do something. There is always a future moment that we will study later. They will not work in the given time. It can occur at any time, but it typically does so during the student years. Therefore, we must begin shutting down all possibilities that cause us as students to procrastinate. What are the primary goals of students engaging in procrastination? What genuinely prompts individuals to put things off? These are the questions that should be answered.

What constitutes procrastination in students?

Many students are facing procrastination in their lives, with or without knowing it. There are distinct reasons why a student might start procrastinating. Some of them are:

Perfectiveness

Some students hold themselves to extremely ambitious standards. They had unrealistic expectations. They think that everything should be done flawlessly and without any mistakes. If they are not perfectionists, they will see no reason to begin the task at all. This kind of thinking is mostly to blame for procrastination. A person is still a human, and it is okay for them to make mistakes. What counts is the effort you put forth. It would be best if you adopted a unique perspective. You will not face criticism for not being a perfectionist. You can be lenient with yourself.

Students Fear of Not Passing

Their fear is the second reason they put things off. Competition amongst students can be fierce. Some students are so afraid they will not succeed or live up to expectations. They fear failing at a task. The need to avoid possible failure causes students to put off completing their tasks until later.

No Motivation

When students do not see the value of a task or do not fully comprehend a topic, they may need more drive to begin or finish it. Anybody who wants to succeed must maintain their motivation. It is critical to maintain motivation, particularly throughout the initial years of education, to stay consistent.

Challenges with their tasks

Some students need help with the tasks. Students may procrastinate as a coping mechanism for the tension and anxiety brought on by work that seems too hard or overwhelming. So, they became too lazy to complete that task.

Undefined Goals

A significant contributing factor is that certain students need more goals and ambitions. Students need more certainty about their plans, activities, and subject selection. It is easier for students to put off assignments when there are unclear goals because they find it difficult to understand why they are there. Establishing specific goals for learners to strive for in the future is important. Establishing a well-defined path toward achieving your goals is important because it will shape your future.

Habits of Procrastination

While we may first dismiss procrastination, students may eventually develop a difficult-to-break habit out of it. Students will eventually establish a tendency to put off assignments and their work. They will begin reacting negatively to challenging situations automatically.

Ineffective time management and routine

Students who start procrastinating usually need a schedule or timetable that shows them where they are wasting their time. Their daily schedule becomes so disorganized that they are still determining what to do with their life. They appear to be spending their lives instead of living in it. It is another reason for procrastination. A student should have a set schedule and routine so they can live their lives in a way that balances their studies and leisure time.

Lack of awareness of Consequences

Some students put off doing assignments because they do not think that waiting around will have an adverse effect. Although the effects will not be felt right away, they could ruin their future. With their own hands, they will be killing their future. They will not experience it right away. On the other hand, postponed effects, like low marks, can affect future and long-term academic progress. Although some students fail to see it, it is crucial to concentrate on actions that have the potential to lead to success.

CHAPTER 2

THE NEGATIVE EFFECTS OF PROCRASTINATION

As we learned in the first chapter, students may suffer negative consequences by procrastinating. It may have consequences that endanger their future. There are numerous repercussions that a student may experience. Furthermore, students frequently still need to understand the long-term effects of their procrastination. This chapter discusses the potential consequences students may encounter to help them correct their course before it gets too late. After learning what causes procrastination in students and how to deal with those situations, it is important to assess your choices for your bright future and yourself. It is important to have a full understanding of this topic. These are a few of the repercussion's procrastination can have on a student.

1: Missing Possibilities for the future

You put together your future towards brightness during your time as a student. At the beginning of their accomplishment, students are presented with many opportunities. Missed opportunities, including applying for scholarships, internships, or other programs, might be caused by procrastination. How can a student apply for a job if they do not know the essential qualifications? You get devoid of essential things when you procrastinate. The world of today is a capable one. Because of your lack of interest in the past, someone with strong abilities will ultimately take your place if you have none.

Delaying assignments might also cause students to lose out on important extracurricular or educational opportunities. For laying the foundation for the future, it might be a huge setback.

2: Delayed growth on a personal level

You start experiencing your own personal growth—body, mind, and soul—when you are a teenager. Procrastination can hinder your personal development. Students might pass up chances to learn about themselves. Their interests will not be able to be pursued. They will not be able to advance intellectually or personally. The development of fundamental life skills will remain unfinished.

3: Negative health impacts

It is a fact that you will deal with mental health issues throughout your life as a student somehow. If they are working hard and consistently, they will feel more relaxed. However, procrastination will increase your stress and anxiety levels as a student. Additionally, procrastination causes worry and anxiety and can be detrimental to one's physical and mental well-being. A sedentary lifestyle, bad eating habits, and sleep deprivation can all lead to a reduction in one's general state of well-being, which includes mental and physical health.

4: Problems with Self-Esteem

It could make you feel low about yourself. You will begin to doubt your own abilities. Students who consistently put off doing things can suffer from low self-esteem and confidence. Students who procrastinate often end up performing poorly in every area of their lives. This unpleasant loop could demotivate them and make them think they cannot achieve academic success. At that moment, you will inevitably fail because it might be incredibly challenging to overcome confidence and self-esteem.

5: Prolonged Consequences

Enjoying life is extremely crucial for students, particularly in this Generation Z period. However, we cannot ignore the reality that procrastination will ultimately turn into a habit outside of the classroom. At first, it will not have any effects, but with time, it will begin to interfere with both your personal and professional life. You will need help to learn time management techniques. It will, therefore, become quite challenging to overcome procrastination. It is essential to give yourself a reality check on your future and the achievements you want to achieve in a variety of spheres of life.

6: Tense interpersonal relationships

Your parents have high expectations for you, but a student in their initial teenage year will never notice. It is quite acceptable for them to see their kid as the world's greatest. Have you ever considered how your actions may affect and offend your parents and other loved ones? Your connections with others may suffer because of procrastination. If the student who is delaying is often stressed out or unavailable because of last-minute work, your friends and family can also be impacted. Additionally, it may hinder your ability to interact with others, particularly in collaborative tasks where team members may get irritated by delays. You will destroy not only yourself but also other people.

Apart from them, there exist other significant ramifications like poor academic achievement, skills development, and more. Now that we are aware of every consequence, let us ask with a bit more realism.

Will there ever be a time when procrastinating can help you as a student?

Now that the ways procrastination can negatively impact a student's life have been thoroughly discussed, you might wonder if procrastination is beneficial, considering how automatic it can be. It is a question that a teenager might ask themselves. Given that nature gave us a procrastinating brain, it cannot be all that horrible, can it? Since we are talking about this subject, we have learned that procrastination is a habit. There must be an evolutionary benefit to continuing the habit of procrastination, as it has been a human behavior from ancient civilizations to the present. So, in my opinion, based on my knowledge and reflections. For some people, the case may be special, but I believe it will only have negative effects on teenagers. You can never benefit from procrastination. This could have a severe and harmful impact on your future

CHAPTER 3

TAKING BABY STEPS IS NOT A PROBLEM

Now that we know what procrastination is and the unusual ways it can impact your life, let us move on.

Acknowledging that, yes, there is a problem.

We must understand that developing coping mechanisms is necessary for mental stability. Realizing that procrastination is happening in your life is the first step toward changing it. Accept it in your mind. Just imagine the following scenario. Act as though you are reflecting on your life. After reflecting, you acknowledge that your behaviors are impacting your life. At this point, you or any other student will become quite irritated and "try" to convince themselves that everything is under control and nothing is wrong. The more you feel that you are perfect but that everything in your life is failing, the more upset you become. Because we are only human, this cycle of justifying your actions will continue to occur repeatedly. But carefully consider what you are doing with your life.

Simply acknowledging that, yes, this is happening to me is your first baby step. You must recognize that I must make changes since this is what is happening in my life. Accepting it will help you get a reality check on your life's events. You will be allowed to acknowledge it after you have accepted. Next, admit what is causing you to put things off and prolong your work. Without a doubt, students can procrastinate in a variety of ways.

Acknowledging your Triggers

Prior to starting to change your ways, you should understand that each person has unique triggers. They frequently have feelings of procrastination. It is acceptable to know that certain elements can tend to give students a different trigger for delaying, even if they are busy, avoiders, or perfectionists. While their surroundings and extracurricular activities may heavily impact some students, others may be struggling due to a variety of internal mental and emotional issues. It might be that a student is an adventure seeker. Conversely, there exist people who are Perfectionists and Avoiders, driven by internal mental models of what constitutes worthy work.

Any irrelevant and entertaining hobby that allows students to put off their intended assignment until the last minute can trigger them. They may also be provoked to put off chores by activities that result in procrastination. You must understand yourself what your triggers are as a student, and then you will have the will to work on them. It is acceptable to begin making small improvements. Nothing is changeable in an instant. It may require some time, and you must convince yourself that everything will be all right. You should also acknowledge that putting off tasks is a habit that develops over time. Look for your habits and accept the impact they are having on your life. You ought to be aware of the detrimental effects it has on your well-being, productivity, academic standing, and student life.

What are the Strategies for recognizing that you are engaging in procrastination?

For those who are truthful with themselves, they are likely aware of when they are engaging in procrastination. For certainty, however, look at these points to determine if you are engaging in procrastination.

These are some strategies for recognizing that you are engaging in procrastination. The following are some beneficial signs that will assist you in recognizing situations in which you are engaging in procrastination.

1. It is true that you are engaging in procrastination if you decide to spend your day working on low-priority items from your Do List rather than focusing on your most important tasks or assignments.

2. When it comes to your schoolwork, you are reading your e-mails or messages multiple times, but you do not commence to work on them. In the unlikely event that you begin to make decisions regarding what you are going to do with them, I am sad to inform you that you have a pattern of doing so.

3. The moment you sit down to begin a high-priority school assignment, you almost instantly begin engaging in enjoyable things such as playing games or participating in other enjoyable activities.

4. If you are a student and you are Leaving a task unfinished despite the fact that you are aware of its significance. You

have procrastination in your life. You still ignore it like a plague.

5. As teenagers, students are quite immature. They do lack focus. Rather than focusing on your schoolwork, you are frequently responding with "Yes" to things not significant and requested by others.

6. If you are studying based on how you are feeling, then this is it for you. One's work ought to be a top priority. If you are waiting for the "right mood" or "right time" to tackle the crucial task, then this is another poor habit that you should try to eradicate.

You could find that these assist you better grasp who you are. To begin, you might want to consider beginning a notebook in which you will record the thoughts, feelings, or circumstances that are associated with your procrastination. Keep an eye out for patterns as time passes. This is the beginning of the entire process of beginning your journey. Consider that overcoming your tendency to put things off requires time. It is all right to take your time. It is important to realize that it is appropriate to seek aid from trusted others, such as instructors, peers, or counselors. Use some time and patience to experiment with a few different strategies and determine which one works best for you. While you are establishing new patterns, remember to be patient with yourself.

CHAPTER 4

BE REALISTIC IN YOUR THINKING

In this chapter, I will tell you about a realistic mindset. If you are alive and making it through each day, you have accomplished something. Achieving even the most basic self-care skills, such as getting dressed, brushing our teeth, riding a bike, or driving a car, is progress. We were content with the trivial things that come with growing up as kids because our expectations were not as high. As we mature, we begin to experience heightened expectations, both from those closest to us and from within. In many cases, the level of satisfaction we feel with our achievements is directly correlated to the standards we set for ourselves.

First, ask yourself from where these expectations originate. Other questions you must ask yourself are, "When will I be good enough?" or "What have I accomplished?" or ' Are you in the right direction with your expectations.' Are my expectations too high for you to become a barrier to your success?

This fundamental desire to make a difference in the world and your life is particularly common among students and young adults since they are just starting to take charge of their own lives and make changes. The question of whether we still need this motivation or if our more general or specific aspirations fulfill us arises as we mature.

Perhaps we begin to ponder these questions as we grow older, but it would be wise for students to think about it because they might be tempted to act hastily, leading them to regret their actions later on.

Why can being unrealistic lead to procrastination?

A significant number of students are struggling with the problem of procrastination. They are so much a part of that circle that, after experiencing a great deal of failure, they come to the conclusion that they do, in fact, desire a change in their lives. There is a possibility that you are one of those individuals who is thinking, "Yes, I am done with this bizarre situation, and I need to change my life in order to make it better."

As a result of adopting this mentality, you may have decided to make certain changes in your life that are goal-oriented. Even after you have altered your mentality, you may still find yourself in a position where you are unsuccessful. Your expectations may be so high that you end up quitting your job because you are unable to continue doing it since it is not going according to your will. It could be the case because your expectations are too high or unrealistic. The following are some of the reasons why people procrastinate because of high expectations:

Procrastination is a complicated behavior with several underlying causes; having high expectations is just one of many aspects that might impact your procrastination. Procrastination could be a result of having too many high expectations. Setting lofty goals for yourself is typically accompanied by apprehension of falling short of those standards. Anxieties about falling short might be so great that people procrastinate until the last minute. Your goals may be too ambitious. When you set your sights high, it's easy to feel overwhelmed. If you're overwhelmed by the enormity of your own expectations or simply don't know how to begin tackling a large project, you may find yourself putting it off till later. It will result in procrastination. Maybe you have an obsession with detail. Your perfectionism, in which you hold yourself to an impossible level, may be associated with your high aspirations. When you worry that you will not be able to do anything perfectly, you can put off beginning or finishing the activity at hand. These can be the reason why you are not observing any changes in yourself and are still procrastinating.

The ways in which being realistic can assist you in overcoming procrastination.

1. Having a mindset that is grounded in reality and having expectations that are practical for both you and your future is one solution that you may implement to address this issue. As a student, having a mindset that is realistic in reality can give you the ability to conquer your tendency to put things off till later, improve your academic achievement, and develop a more positive approach to learning for yourself. If you are struggling with procrastination, adopting a realistic outlook will give you a powerful intervention.

2. Understanding and accepting your flaws is the second and most fundamental step. You are able to lessen the paralyzing fear that is linked with perfectionism by viewing mistakes as opportunities for progress rather than failures. The adoption of this mentality will help to cultivate resiliency and will encourage a proactive attitude to the process of learning. You can engage with your job with the assurance that each mistake puts you one step

closer to mastery rather than delaying things on purpose in order to prevent the possibility of making mistakes.

3. The creation of goals that are within one's reach is yet another essential way in which realism combats procrastination. Create a goal that is attainable and feasible for you to reach. By establishing attainable goals, you will be able to align your goals with your current capabilities and the resources that are at your disposal. Instead of giving in to the strain of impossible ambitions, you can break down projects into achievable steps that are within their reach. This mindset will allow you to avoid giving in to the pressure.

4. Your healthy sense of self-assessment is intimately connected to your level of realism. When it comes to overcoming procrastination, one of the most important things you can do is acknowledge both your strengths and the areas in which you may improve. In order to have a more accurate assessment of your capabilities, it is important to establish reasonable expectations for yourself. Self-assurance in your ability to fulfill the requirements of your academic endeavors will be bolstered because of this.

5. Because you are a realistic student, you will be able to understand the significance of getting support and making use of the resources that are available to you. When you feel that you are not adequately prepared to fulfill your academic duties, you are more likely to engage in procrastination. Having a realistic mindset will motivate

you to evaluate your requirements and take measures to fulfill them proactively.

CHAPTER 5

SETTING PRIORITIES

Having a realistic mentality was discussed in the last chapter. Now, let us look at how you are making priorities. First, let us discuss the major understanding of priorities.

Why making priorities is important?

Everything is becoming too difficult. The world is changing drastically. In an ever-changing and challenging setting, students encounter excessive competition daily. Indeed, things are always changing, yet the prospect of change can be terrifying. Adaptation is the only constant. Ask yourself the question of what gives you that fright, though. I understand we shudder at thinking of taking a chance or facing the unknown. However, have you ever considered why it is so hard for us to implement our decisions? Some individuals are always rearranging their priorities. What gives certain people the gift of transformation while you are struggling mightily?

Furthermore, everyone has their own unique set of priorities. You determine your own priorities. Perhaps you prioritize quality time with your loved ones more than focusing on your studies.

Setting priorities is an essential part of a student's life; that much is certain. Your academic performance could be affected. Being able to recognize and prioritize your tasks is crucial. A student's life can be drastically improved with this skill. Always recognize that if you want to transcend your abilities, Priorities must be established. Priority setting has the power over your academic performance and future opportunities, so you should know your priorities. In the long run, it can improve your health and can help you grow as an individual personality. We should also know that knowing what matters most in determining our priorities can alter our future. You need to focus on what will move you closer to your objectives and set priorities accordingly. Over time, it ought to yield the greatest benefits for you.

Why should you set your priorities?

Since your education will shape your future, it is crucial that you prioritize your studies at this age as a student in case of procrastination. These are a few advantages that might help in convincing.

1. First, it will give you goal-oriented behavior and personal growth.

2. You may make efficient use of your time and resources by establishing priorities. Students frequently have to balance conflicting demands on their time. It is difficult to balance and ensure that important chores are finished on time when no defined priorities exist.

3. You can concentrate on the most crucial tasks by determining your priorities. It can help you avoid feeling overburdened and anxious.

4. Your time management abilities will improve. Time management and prioritization are closely related concepts. It will support your achievement in your studies.

5. Giving directions can be greatly aided by it. Establishing priorities will help you feel more focused and oriented.

6. You are a person with various interests, passions, and responsibilities in addition to being a learner. Establishing priorities can assist you in striking a balance between your academic endeavors, relationships, and self-care.

What your priorities should be as a student?

Students who do not set priorities may find themselves procrastinating. The possibility of decision exhaustion is why establishing priorities can cause procrastination. You may have to make a lot of decisions every day. You may find it challenging to organize your assignments, determine which topics to spend more time on and determine how to manage your personal and academic obligations. Thus, learning to set and manage priorities is necessary to break this procrastination. Students' priority responsibilities can change depending on their unique situation, academic standing, and personal objectives. But there are a few routine chores that ought to take precedence over others.

To help you understand what your top priorities should be and how to handle them, let us explore how we might divide priorities into sectors.

Priorities according to your academic standing

Your academics should come first if you want to accomplish your ambitions. Your academic standing should be your primary concern. Maintain a schedule. Possess your whole attendance. You should have the ability to comprehend course material, communicate with professors, and get questions answered in class, depending on your regular attendance and active involvement. Prioritize assignments with deadlines to ensure you turn them in on time and retain your grades. You should concentrate on your studies and upcoming final exams. It can be beneficial to assemble and form a community of people that can support you academically. Communicate effectively with others.

Priorities for your future planning

Put your attention on establishing a long-term professional goal. Therefore, it is essential to determine the steps you will take to accomplish them. An example of this would be concentrating on exploring other job paths. You should go to job fairs and get advice from career services since they can assist you in understanding your future and can help you make better decisions. You should make it a point to network with professionals and investigate the various job options that could be appropriate for you in future. Obtaining some hands-on experience is also preferable. Regarding this, you have the option of participating in internships or working part-time in the relevant field. In addition to aiding in the enhancement of your resume, it will also present you with vital insights that go beyond the classroom.

Your well-being is also important.

Prioritize your physical health as part of your overall well-being. Include a healthy diet, frequent exercise, and enough sleep. It matters for both your academic achievement and general well-being. Monitor your emotional well-being and, if necessary, seek assistance or counseling. Determine your stress management strategies. Participate in extracurricular activities in addition to studying to prevent burnout. Be available for your hobbies, relaxation, and enjoyable leisure activities while juggling your studies, career, and overall health.

CHAPTER 6

PLAN OUT YOUR TIMETABLE

Considering what we discussed in the last chapter regarding priorities, providing sufficient time to all is crucial. Many of you who are reading this, I am sure, are having trouble keeping up with sometimes too many obligations and responsibilities. Some of you might have simply given up because you are so exhausted.

Keeping to a strict schedule can be challenging for students. Not being able to manage your time well is a major contributor to procrastination. You may find yourself continually juggling many tasks when you are a student. Participating in class, finishing homework, and preparing for tests simultaneously is possible. Let us imagine that you have studied more and worked harder in the past.

You force yourselves to spend the entire night studying for exams. You must even put off time-consuming tasks like sleeping and eating to finish your academic work. Without learning to manage your time, you attempted to do everything even when there was too much to do. That is a strategy that will undoubtedly drive you towards failure and frustration. You were so frustrated you had to give up some time along the line. That is not the way, though. If no students have realized that it is their fault, now is the perfect opportunity for them to start practicing better time management. You ought to be proficient in time management. Your health is also something you cannot compromise on. Whatever the obstacles you face, the key to your success is a clear, uncomplicated organizational structure. As a student, you should remember that time is an extremely valuable and scarce resource. Your academic achievement is greatly affected by your time management skills. Your personal growth and general health can also be impacted by it. The key to their success, productivity, and future achievements lies in understanding the significance of time.

How Effective Time Management Can Benefit You?

You can complete more work in less time using a time-management system that works for you. Organizing your life and academics can help you accomplish your priorities and goals: more free time, better grades, a less hectic life, or academic strain.

» Prioritizing things important to you is made easier with an efficient time-management system.

» Having the ability to manage time will assist you in estimating the time needed for each task. You can keep track of how much time you spend on it.

» Knowing how much each task will take and knowing you have the time to complete it will help you avoid becoming frustrated and procrastinating.

» Being in control of a portion of your day enables you to be adaptable during the remaining time. Even keeping track of all your tasks, deadlines, appointments, errands, and reminders in one location is beneficial.

» It helps you be sure that no more than two or three appointments are made simultaneously. You will not experience scheduling issues.

» It can assist you in avoiding feelings of guilt. After you set aside time to study, it is far easier to put it off. If you do not have a strategy to complete your tasks, they may continue to loom over you even when you are not actively engaged in them.

» You might become a well-planned, focused, and time-efficient person who can spend and get better marks in less time by studying.

Let us get started with it.

You cannot just bolt towards your goal right away. You must first determine where you will start and where you are standing right now. Determine the distance between you and what you want to achieve. To find it, you only need to redesign your existing regimen. You must check your timetable and change it for more effective results. Several plans let you be flexible. I think any suggestions can be modified to fit your requirements. You might begin with what works best for you. Whether you live in a dorm, share housing with some other class fellow, or live with your loved ones, you can manage your time according to your will. If you are ready to change it, it shows that you are willing to put in small efforts, and it will work for you. There are various approaches to planning and organizing your schedule. I am happy to recommend that you truly be available to study.

First, you should reevaluate how much time you spend in each of the other areas and if it is evident that you are not managing your time well. Keep in mind that sometimes sacrifices are necessary. You may have to shorten your commute or work fewer hours for fun-related activities. Whatever the case, for your future, you must adapt to solutions.

Together, let us help you become more sensible. Making your own chart is one thing you can do. Note down in intervals of fifteen minutes. Jot down your current routine of activities. Then, keep a log of everything you do, including where you spend your time and what you are doing. I suggest you chart them for the whole week, including the weekend.

You will be able to notice where you spend the additional hour or two you get each day and what you prioritize, doing pleasurable things or studying. You can take advantage of this reality check by wondering how to make the most of your idle time rather than just staring at it. Then, construct a chart showing how to better utilize this "dead" time, and you will have all the time you require. It can assist you in making efficient use of your time.

Setting a schedule according to your will.

Getting a handle on how to organize your life and your studies right now is vitally essential to your achievements in the future. Learning how to organize your life and your academics is not only a good notion; it is the right thing to do at any level, from high school to college or any other level. After understanding the significance of schedules in the last chapter, I hope you can realize that your timetable is the only thing that will allow you to exist. Trust me. You have not even thought about how hectic life may be for you until you start planning for your life.

Your presence at this point in the book indicates that you are attempting to acquire the knowledge necessary to study precisely at this moment. You may be a student who is just beginning to feel overwhelmed. You might be attending classes while caring for a family or balancing five classes plus a part-time job. Both scenarios are possible. These are the primary reasons why people procrastinate. To ensure your success and future, it is essential to have a straightforward schedule to adhere to. You are still willing to make it, which is yet another step up the stairs of success, despite saying that you simply do not have the time to schedule, list, and record yourself. Making a well-thought-out plan or schedule for your study time is the surest method to guarantee that you will cover all the material necessary to pass the exam and perhaps even do well. It asks you to think about your current situation and abilities, how much time you will need to become competent enough to pass the exam, and how much more time you will need to complete the tasks required to acquire a high score if you want to get that score. So, to plan your preparation effectively, you must be aware of your learning ability, present circumstances, and desired outcomes. Then and only then can you make a plan that will give you a better shot at accomplishing your goals.

It is okay to get help.

Imagine for a second that you have upcoming exams; how do you plan to manage your time?

Due to the required time, unexpected events and crises may certainly arise occasionally, regardless of how well you organize your timetable. As a result, you should not set a firm deadline for when you will study for your examinations. It ought to be an adaptable document that changes with your situation. Your preparation tasks intended due dates, and actual performance relative to those dates should be clearly displayed in a high-quality schedule organizer. Make a note on the organizer of any schedule adjustments you made based on your actual performance.

CHAPTER 7

MAKE USE OF THE POMODORO EFFECT

In this chapter I will tell you about Pomodoro effect.

What is the Pomodoro effect?

You live in a world of academics that moves quickly. Students frequently have an excessive number of assignments, projects, and deadlines to meet. Procrastination is your go-to behavior when you cannot handle managing your time. As we discovered in the last chapter, effective time management is essential to your future academic success. There are various strategies you can use to stay online and break your procrastinating tendencies. The Pomodoro method is one of them. The Pomodoro Method is one well-liked and extensively accepted strategy that has the potential to transform your life completely. Francesco Cirillo developed it in the latter part of the 1980s. This time management technique has grown in favor due to its effectiveness and simplicity. This method can assist you in overcoming procrastination, but you must first understand how it can benefit you personally. You must first familiarize yourself with the fundamentals of the Pomodoro Technique. You need to understand how it will help you as a student and how it will increase productivity and decrease stress.

How is the Pomodoro Technique used?

Now that you know the term Pomodoro, let us talk about how it functions. This technique is based on segmenting work into smaller, more manageable chunks. You must create intervals, typically 25 minutes long and interspersed with brief pauses.

These intervals are known as "Pomodoros," Inspired by Cirillo's original tomato-shaped kitchen timer, this term is named after the Italian word for tomato. Once you have finished your four Pomodoros, you can take a longer 15–30-minute break. In this manner, you will be able to focus better and take breaks. This method will help you to increase your productivity and focus by instilling a sense of urgency in the allotted time slots.

» To grasp it more thoroughly, let us divide it into manageable steps.

» Choose a single task that you wish to work on before anything else. Anything from your study could be the source.

» As your "first" Pomodoro interval, set a twenty-five-minute timer.

» For those twenty-five minutes, give your full attention to the assigned work.

» After the allotted 25 minutes, take a 5-minute rest. Consider it a prize for your diligence.

» Return to the assignment for a further twenty-five minutes after the little break. You are free to use "Pomodoro" as often as you like.

» Take a lengthy vacation following four Pomodoro's.

Additionally, you are free to modify it as you see fit.

In what way does it benefit you against procrastination?

This Pomodoro Technique will continue to be an invaluable tool in your quest for both career and personal success. This technique can be a flexible and useful tool to improve time management and productivity. Its advantages go beyond the immediate domain of work fulfillment; it impacts multiple facets of your general welfare. Through enhanced concentration, less procrastination, and avoiding burnout, the Pomodoro Technique enables people to take charge of their work routines and attain a more favorable work-life equilibrium. You can keep navigating the challenges of your contemporary life by using it. This method has some advantages that affect mental health, general productivity, and emotional stability differently. Let us examine the many benefits of the Pomodoro Technique in this post and see how it can greatly enhance your work habits and way of life.

Keeping you from developing procrastination habits.

Procrastination is a widespread issue that many people deal with. You can overcome this problem using the Pomodoro Technique, which divides work into smaller, easier-to-manage pieces. The brief time allotted to each Pomodoro can help you feel less overwhelmed by the task at hand. You will not be able to put off starting and finishing tasks as easily.

It will support you in becoming more productive.

The Pomodoro Technique will help you develop a feeling of urgency. The pressure to finish on time can be a strong incentive for you. It will motivate you to produce quality work. It will assist you in finishing assignments within the specified time limits. Your overall productivity will rise significantly as a result of multiple Pomodoros.

Makes you feel like you have accomplished something.

When you break down huge activities into more manageable portions, you will feel a sense of accomplishment with each Pomodoro that you complete. As you take these small steps, you will find that they help you develop a more optimistic outlook. It will encourage you to continue working more diligently than before. It will be possible for you to keep a feeling of accomplishment throughout the day.

No longer experiencing feelings of exhaustion.

When it comes to minimizing burnout, the incorporation of short breaks in between Pomodoros can be an essential component for you to consider. Pauses that are brief and frequent will allow you to refresh your mind. Stress and weariness will be reduced as a result of this. You will remain stable throughout the day if you maintain a healthy balance between the work you do and the rest you take.

Provides you with a heightened awareness of time.

If you use Pomodoros regularly, you will better understand the passage of time. Because of this heightened awareness of time, you will have a deeper comprehension of the situation. You will be able to comprehend how certain intervals can be utilized to accomplish a great deal. It will improve your ability to estimate time and plan accordingly.

Aids in keeping a harmonious balance between your personal and professional life:

The Pomodoro Technique encourages a healthy equilibrium between work and leisure time. You can prevent engaging in prolonged periods of continuous work, which can contribute to burnout, by combining shorter breaks and longer rest intervals into your schedule. Maintaining this equilibrium will enhance your general well-being and sense of fulfillment.

CHAPTER 8

UTILIZING THE TIME-BLOCKING TECHNIQUES

We covered the Pomodoro technique in the previous chapter. Now, let's talk about another technique that might help you avoid procrastinating and develop new learning habits to attain a brighter future. For any subject to be understood, your method of studying is essential. Let us talk about another study aid that may be useful to you.

Organizing your day into discrete time slots for certain tasks will help you maintain a disciplined and targeted approach to your academic work and personal life. Another time-management strategy is time blocking, which sets aside particular time slots for various projects or pursuits. This strategy lets you prioritize your chores and manage your time more effectively. It also improves your general output.

Comprehending Time Blocking.

With time blocking, you can set up designated periods for various jobs, endeavors, or pursuits. Depending on the task's complexity and nature, these blocks might last anything from a few hours to as little as fifteen minutes. You will minimize interruptions and distractions by concentrating only on the allocated task during each allotted block of time.

These are some tactics to use the time block method. Put them into practice during your study session to achieve success and prevent procrastination.

Identifying your goal.

Using time-blocking tactics involves several phases, one of which is determining your objective. First, list your short- and long-term career and personal goals. All you need to do is rank these objectives in order of significance and urgency.

Breaking this objective.

After identifying your main goal, break these objectives down into more doable, smaller tasks. It is now simpler to set up particular time slots for every task.

Select the length of time you want.

Recognize when you are most energetic and understand your daily routine. During these times, assign the most significant and taxing responsibilities. It may continue for a few hours.

Putting together a schedule.

Make a visual timetable of your work using a planner, calendar, or other specialized time management tool, then allocate tasks by it.

Taking pauses throughout.

You ought to Incorporate brief intervals between time slots to avoid fatigue and sustain efficiency.

Modifications.

Examine your time-blocking plan on a regular basis. Evaluate what went well and what needs to be improved. Modify your schedule in response to shifting priorities, unforeseen circumstances, or changing objectives.

Flexibilities.

Time blocking is an adaptable method. Try out various lengths and arrangements to see what suits you the best. Be prepared to modify and improve your strategy in light of your experiences and evolving situations.

Advantages of using the time block method.

The strategy of time blocking might give you a variety of advantages over other approaches. Among these advantages are the following:

1. People can focus on a single activity at a time, which reduces the need to multitask.

2. Better outcomes will be within your reach.

3. It encourages "deep work," a condition of hyper-focus that improves efficiency and output.

4. Instead of putting off important tasks until later, you can take a proactive approach to time management using this method.

5. If you give yourself a certain amount of time to complete a task, you are more likely to get right to work.

6. Although time blocking offers structure, it also leaves room for maneuverability.

7. Goals are better aligned with tasks when time is blocked.

8. Being aware that there are certain times when people have a plan for their days, they may consider their energy and focus levels when deciding when to get things done.

Blocking your time can help reduce the tension of having a thorough list of things to complete.

9. It will assist you in maintaining a regular schedule. Time blocking is a wonderful way to get into a pattern and stay on top of your work.

10. It helps you feel more predictable and consistent. Feeling accomplished and fulfilled is the result of finishing activities within the allotted time. A rise in contentment with one's work life may result from this kind of reinforcement.

A brief declaration.

I would like to bring to your attention a common mistake that many students make, which is that they apply the same instructional strategies to each task or subject. There are a lot of different strategies that can assist you in overcoming procrastination; nevertheless, to be sure, you should use the strategy that is beneficial to you and that strategy on which you can get reliable results. Make an effort to determine which method is most effective for you, and then work towards achieving your goals. Keep in mind that a curious mind benefits from engaging in experimentation.

CHAPTER 9

GET RID OF INTERRUPTIONS

In this chapter, I will tell you about some of the more practical aspects. One of them is the setting where you are studying.

So, you are devoting time and energy to your studies, but you are still finding fault with something. When you sit down to study, do you enjoy being there? Also, it is optimistic, right?

> » Has lightning ever caught your attention? Is it bright enough? Does it seem too light or too dark? How does your study environment make you feel?

> » Have you gathered everything you will need before studying?

Even when you focused intently, you might not have noticed all of this before. A student's study space plays a crucial role in helping them remain committed to their goals. The environment in which one chases knowledge has a significant influence on one's learning outcomes and overall academic success. It says something about his priorities and the level of commitment he has to his studies. The environment has a big impact on students' motivation, crucial skill development, and thinking processes. The probability of procrastination is greatly affected by the physical location that a student prefers to study. A student may find it easier to procrastinate if their study space is unorganized since it can contribute to their feelings of being overwhelmed and diversions. How can a student set up his workspace for studying? It is something on which students ought to concentrate.

Let us now take a moment to really consider how a student might satisfy his study obligations by making the most of his options in life.

Methods for creating a conducive study space.

Having the following tactics will help you stay focused on your studies.

1. your own unique preference.

You are the one who will struggle against your habits. You are the one battling for a prosperous future. If you adjust to your unique preferences, that is good.

First and foremost, you must acknowledge and adjust to your own learning preferences. Those preferences will aid your ability to contribute to a more flexible environment. It is possible that you will do your best in total quiet. It can be that you prefer having background music. Customize your surroundings according to your will. Find out what you want. Adjust your space so that it meets all your students' requirements for a comfortable and focused learning environment.

2: Maintain simplicity.

Realize that the most efficient settings are usually the most basic ones, so before you go out and purchase hundreds of markers, pencils, binders, and folders, stop and consider your options. Wisely, the order in which you organize your books, notebooks, and notes should correspond with the way you think. Have all the study aids you will need nearby. Pens, notepads, textbooks, and any other materials you regularly utilize are included in this.

3: Order and Neatness.

A well-kept study area lessens visual distractions and encourages mental focus. Have all your study resources in one location, arranged tastefully and conveniently. A student's mind will remain easily focused when materials are freely accessible, and the study environment is clear of excessive clutter.

4: Ease of movement.

Feeling at ease in that environment is another crucial factor. Insufficient lighting or uncomfortable seats might both lead to your pain. It will make it simpler to continue procrastinating. Make sure your chair and workstation are properly configured to provide you with useful support.

5: Remove any distractions.

Distractions can derail you and lead to procrastination. As far as possible, keep it peaceful and free of interruptions so that you can concentrate. If you're trying to focus but can't help but look at or respond to your phone, it's easier and more productive to just take it away.

6: Enchantment in the lighting.

Flexible and adaptable learning environments are also conducive to students' best learning outcomes. Burnout may result from a student experiencing rigidity in his studies. It is vital to create an atmosphere in which procrastinating cannot be used as a coping strategy. You can receive that assistance from lightning. During the day, pay attention to having the space in natural light. If you are a night owl, invest in an adjustable lamp so you can have a bright place to read and write at night. It makes sense to create a space with complete lighting since you will be in here for a long time, allowing you to properly relax and concentrate on the tasks at hand.

7: Make clear rules.

Before you dive headfirst into your academics, there are some personal priorities you should establish, such as being available for your loved ones. Get the word out to your loved ones—especially your friends—about how serious you are about your studies. Prove to them how significant this moment is. Explain to them that you will be unable to participate at certain times because they are reserved for your study. Studying does not have to interfere with your relationships if you know how to manage your time wisely. Establish the ground rules that I will be studying and spending time with my loved ones during this period.

8: Make your choice of study symbol.

Treat it as an enjoyable activity where you can select an item that you can link to your academic pursuits. As an example, consider an item like a cap or scarf. You're even welcome to have one of those adorable trolls as a desk accessory. Simply place the troll on top of your desk or put on the hat whenever you need to concentrate. As a bonus, it can "get you in the mood" to study and even alert those around you that you are busy at work. Remember that your symbol is only to be used in relation to study. The meaning of your study symbol is misunderstood. It should be used with caution.

A side note especially for you.

Always remember that You must spend more money to have a higher-quality desk lamp, or you might need to reconsider your study arrangement entirely. The ideal setting corresponds to an environment built for learning. It should have fewer interruptions and good equipment. Being well-prepared is not just a matter of keeping things neat only. If you want to maintain the interior environment, you must age the exterior environment. Keeping things neat will eventually give you a sense of motivation to work on your assignments and deadlines. It will help you to give a push. So, for your fight against procrastination, these might help you a lot.

CHAPTER 10

YOUR SURROUNDINGS ARE VERY IMPORTANT

In the last chapter, we learned about how we may eliminate disturbances from our environments and the ways in which we can create a conducive environment for learning. In addition, we learned about other individuals' interference in our educational pursuits at the very end. They can play a huge part in overcoming your Procrastination. As a result, the entirety of this chapter will be devoted to discussing how the people in your immediate environment can impact you and how you can deal with it.

How can positive individuals in your life help you fight against Procrastination?

Interactions with various people are unavoidable in the various settings of a student's life. These people, who can be mentors, friends, professors, and classmates, greatly impact how a student develops personally and academically. They can help in your fight against Procrastination. Let us count the number of people you interact with daily.

Let's take a broad stance and observe. Your interactions will mostly be categorized into three groups of people. Your loved ones, family, friends, and parents will all be there. People in your academic setting and the final category are uncommon scenarios we will address at the end of the chapter since they are unavoidable.

Let's start by assessing how these characterized people around you can support you.

Providing you with moral, emotional, and social support.

A student's emotional health greatly depends on his social network, which should be kind and helpful. Exam pressure, meeting deadlines, and other academic life obstacles can be too much for you to handle. Put yourself in the company of positive individuals. Maintain an environment of understanding people around you. They should be able to provide you with a feeling of acceptance and be the source of your vital emotional stability. It might be anyone—your family members for their constant support, your friends for their listening ears, or your mentors for their advice. These relationships will provide emotional support, enhancing your mental health and resilience.

Your brilliant source of motivation.

The people who are in your immediate vicinity have the potential to function as a source of motivation and accountability for you. It is possible for you, as a student, to be inspired to excel academically by studying with other motivated students, participating in conversations with talented teachers, or working together with other students eager to study. Furthermore, being a part of a community that places a high value on education instills a sense of drive to do better. It will motivate you to concentrate on your studies and inspire you to work towards a bright future. It will help in leaving your Procrastination.

Develop your learning capacity.

You can broaden your skill set by interacting with your classmates and teachers, enabling academic collaboration. It will be possible for you to engage in new educational experiences. Group study sessions should be held. Through participation in collaborative projects and classroom discussions, you will have the opportunity to gain learnings from a variety of points of view. Students can widen their understanding and acquire new perspectives by interacting with the people in their immediate environment. Your knowledge will be improved as a result.

New opportunities.

As I said, the people in your immediate surroundings may frequently be trained professionals. Building relationships with instructors can help you have great possibilities for mentorship and future job prospects. These opportunities can be beneficial to you. You will have a greater willingness to network. Through networking, you will be able to expand your professional circle and gain insights into potential career pathways and prospects for internships or job placements.

Managing your relationships.

Now that you understand their significance, you need to be able to navigate relationships with people in both your personal and academic lives. You also need to know how to take care of your academics while managing these relationships. Emotional intelligence, interpersonal skills, and effective communication are all necessary. These are the tactics that will assist you in the future when interacting with those around you. First, Establish clear limits for your personal and academic life. Respectfully convey these boundaries while keeping others' boundaries in mind. Relationships that are balanced and healthy are facilitated by setting and upholding limits. Try interacting with people, and work on your active listening skills. Open and transparent channels of communication should be established with instructors, fellow students, and members of the academic community. Keep your relationship with studies separate from one another.

Be wary of bad company, the third category.

You get easily captivated in your teenage years. You will be drawn to negative things, or perhaps you will be drawn to them because of strange confrontations. There are those who can permanently hurt you and your future, and they are a threat to you. These individuals belong to the third group. The phrase "bad company" usually describes people who act in ways that are harmful to a productive and encouraging learning environment. They might harm your standing at school. Students who are exposed to negative peer pressure may become entangled in extracurricular activities that take them away from their studies. Excessive partying, drug usage, or indulging in activities that divert attention from academic obligations are a few examples of these distractions. You may experience unfavorable peer pressure. They might push you to engage in actions that are inconsistent with your moral principles or impede your ability to succeed academically. This can involve you participating in dangerous behavior like skipping courses or cheating. It may be difficult for you to break free from harmful patterns if you have been exposed to a negative peer group. In these cases, later on, students may be prevented from making constructive adjustments in their lives by their fear of social rejection or judgment. They might be the reason for your Procrastination. Thus, it is critical to exercise caution and stay in your lane right away. Avoid allowing your thoughts to divert you from these kinds of distractions. Just be mindful that the bad individuals in your life cannot harm your future.

CHAPTER 11

ENVISION SUCCEEDING

What is Envisioned for students?

Let us have a thought about something. In this chapter, I will tell you about Envision. For a moment, put yourself in the shoes of your future self. You are experiencing joy. You have arrived at a point in your life when you have achieved your goals and are content. You and your family are enjoying a happy life together. You are working in the field toward your goals. Whatever it was that you desired to accomplish, you have accomplished it. Do you feel that you have finished imagining yourself in the future? Now that you have a visualization of your future, you might be thinking to yourself, "Yes, I have to be that person I saw in my visualization. You must be thinking now that the reason I want to accomplish that objective is so that I can become that ideal version of myself. The power of envisioning in your life is demonstrated here.

Students "envision" is the picture or idea they have in their heads of their future selves, their aspirations, and the things they hope to accomplish. Everything that they hope to achieve and the path they envision for their lives are part of it. To envision is to picture something mentally. Usually, something has to do with one's hopes, dreams, or the eventual result of an effort. It entails forming an idea or picture of one's ideal self in one's mind. External factors, together with one's own interests, values, and life experiences, frequently shape this imaginative process. Students' ability to envisage the future has a significant impact on their aspirations, drive, and perspective on school and life in general.

When trying to combat Procrastination, why is it vital to envision?

Because it may give us a solid foundation of motivation and a distinct feeling of purpose, envisioning is a vital tool for students to use in order to overcome Procrastination during the learning process. Instilling a feeling of purpose, drive, and accountability in yourself as a student can be accomplished through the use of visualization, which gives a psychological framework that can assist you in overcoming Procrastination. When it comes to overcoming Procrastination, visualization can be a fantastic resource because it can provide you with a compelling incentive to take action. It provides you with a distinct road map and a feeling of accountability. By making a connection between the actions you are taking right now and a meaningful future, you, as a student, will have a greater chance of overcoming the habit of putting off duties and constantly working toward achieving your long-term objectives.

Consider the following reasons why visualizing is so important in the context of Procrastination:

Strengthening your forward momentum.

Momentum can be a potent cure for Procrastination because it allows you to experience the satisfactory results of your constant effort. You can experience these impacts.

Get started. In order to develop momentum, taking the baby steps toward a larger vision is essential. A sense of accomplishment is increased with each task that is successfully done. By doing so, you will be inspired to improve yourself and to keep moving forward with your actions.

Goodbye to the pursuit of perfection.

Your tendency to Procrastination can be traced to perfectionism and a fear of failing. Visualization is a tool that can assist you in adopting a growth attitude. You will be able to comprehend the obstacles that you have encountered. These are the steps that you will take to learn something new. Putting your attention on the path that leads to their objective will increase the likelihood that you will be able to conquer your tendency toward perfectionism and the Procrastination that comes after it.

Utilizing Visualization to Achieve Success.

Imagining yourself succeeding and experiencing happy outcomes is an important part of your envisioning. There is a connection between your visualization process and the accomplishment of your goals.

Uplifting your spirits.

You can function as a great motivator with this optimistic picture that you have. Having a positive mental attitude can be achieved by visualizing success. Procrastination will become less appealing to you as a result of this, and you will be reminded of the advantages of taking quick action.

Living your life with a consistent sense of purpose.

One of the most common causes of Procrastination is a lack of any sense of purpose or direction in one's life. Visualization has the potential to give you a distinct feeling of purpose. You will be reminded on a regular basis of the significance of your work and the ways in which you may contribute to the overall vision.

Your propensity to put off completing your chores will decrease if you have an intense sense of purpose.

Motivating factors that are one of a kind.

Because it establishes a connection between your current activities and your long-term objectives, envisioning will give you a sense of purpose. With this connection, you will be able to increase the significance of your tasks. Your internal motivation will be significantly bolstered because of this.

When you are able to recognize the reason behind your behaviors, you will be more likely to take prompt action rather than putting off chores by procrastinating rather than taking immediate action.

How you will manage your time effectively.

Students are able to manage their time effectively. From this point forward, you will be able to prioritize your tasks according to how well they connect with your vision. Having this in place will guarantee that you are concentrating on the things that will contribute to your success in the long run.

Strategy for Reward.

Designing a system of rewards that is dependent on the fulfillment of tasks is one way to envision. Positive reinforcement can be achieved by linking task completion with rewards. Reducing Procrastination, a reward system might help you see work as a chance to achieve positive outcomes.

Do what makes you happy if that is what you like, but do not forget to consider what can dampen or even ruin your mood. Make sure you recognize and monitor both your strengths and areas for improvement if you value this approach. These advantages can be useful to you down the road. Your future self should be your motivation the next time you feel the want to procrastinate. Envision your future self in a situation where they fail and attempt to put yourself in their shoes. Next, consider.

Imagine your future self experiencing all the good emotions that would accompany a successful outcome. Envision your future self in each scenario, down to the smallest detail. To boost your motivation to achieve your vision of success instead of your failure vision, it is helpful to get a taste of the two possible future selves. Get it to stick and have an impact. Keep in mind that this is not wishful thinking but rather a gift of insight into your future. Embrace it and put it to clever use on your path to a brighter tomorrow.

CHAPTER 12

KEEP TRACK OF YOUR NECESSITIES

Going to class, doing homework, participating in extracurriculars, and keeping up with friends are just a few of the many things that students typically have to manage. It might be difficult to keep track of important things like school supplies, personal items, and everyday needs in the middle of all this chaos. Everything a student needs is laid out for them in this book section.

Ways in which students might combat procrastination by maintaining a record of essentials:

Strategically organizing and keeping track of essentials is one efficient strategy to combat procrastination. Keeping track of essentials can be useful in various ways.

1. As a habit, procrastination tends to keep people from getting things done. Delays cause stress, which raises the risk that work quality may decline, ultimately leading to feelings of failure. Tracking needs is the key to breaking this loop.

2. Maintaining a system of regular necessity tracking can help you become more self-disciplined. As a student, you develop habits that encourage self-control and responsibility since you are always involved in planning and organizing.

3. Priorities become more apparent when you maintain tabs on your essentials. This category falls under academic materials, personal responsibilities, and due dates.

4. Setting and creating goals is a fundamental part of necessity tracking. You are more likely to establish

SMART goals—goals that are specific, measurable, realistic, relevant, and have a deadline—if you keep track of your academic and personal needs.

5. You can establish a system of responsibility by recording your essentials. Making a note of when things are due, what needs carrying out, and when you study shows that you are serious about getting things done. Having the plan in writing makes it much easier to remember to get things done.

6. You can make your tasks more doable by tracking what they must have. Tasks and assignments are less intimidating when organized in this way, which reduces the tension that comes with having a mountain of work to do.

7. Maintaining an organized and productive study environment is a natural byproduct of tracking your academic requirements. One way to create an atmosphere that encourages focus and decreases procrastination is to have a well-organized desk, specific places to study, and a systematic way to store things.

Essentials for students to possess.

Being well-organized is crucial for thriving in the hectic and complex college life. By applying these tactics, students can build systems to facilitate tracking academic and personal necessities.

If you want to be a good student, here are some things you need:

1. The first step in maintaining order is selecting an appropriate bag or backpack. Choose a bag with plenty of room and plenty of pockets. It will ensure that everything has a specific place, making finding what you need much easier.

2. Gather important dates for classes, assignments, and extracurriculars, and make a master schedule. Put the calendar on your table and continue to mark it as you go.

3. Establish a specific study area, either at home or on campus. This space needs to be tidy and undisturbed.

4. Put the Two-Minute Rule into Practice. Act without delay if it will take less than two minutes. Following this rule will save you from getting overwhelmed by a pileup of little jobs.

5. Keep a list of things to accomplish and goals to achieve, and review it every day or week. Sort things in order of importance and urgency.

6. Use color-coded stickers or labels to restrict certain topics, items, or rooms in your home. Thanks to this visual signal, things are better organized as a whole, which facilitates identification and classification.

7. The "one in, one out" principle might be useful when buying extra stuff, particularly if it is unnecessary. Donate or delete one old item for every new one you bring in. It aids in avoiding superfluous mess.

8. Think about utilizing see-through storage containers for things stashed in cabinets, bookshelves, or under your mattress.

Reasons why students should practice sound financial management.

As a student, you will probably be spending money. You continue to put things off, procrastinate, and end up spending a lot of money on things that aren't necessary. Therefore, it is wise to plan for financial management and prioritize needs. Some people find it difficult to cut costs. Avoid letting it become an obstacle on the path to success. But this is very necessary if you don't want to run out of money in the next several weeks. Regardless of their interests or financial situation, anybody can benefit from a few innovative solutions that can help them save money on education. Always be aware of where your money is going. Make smart use of it because money is an investment in your present and future selves.

If you are looking for ways to save money while you study, there are a few options to explore. For sure, you will be able to save money with these. Here are a few imaginative suggestions that you might think about:

1. To save money and have enough for school, buying only what you need is wise. Consider whether you need or want the item before buying it. You cannot disregard it as soon as you realize it's a want. You can save money. It will help you gain insight into your future by purchasing only what you need.

2. Your studies really benefit from textbooks. But just because you're trying to save money doesn't mean you can skip out on buying textbooks. Your textbook needs can be met. However, look around for different bookstores to see if you can get better prices for your needed textbooks. You can save money with this because you can purchase high-quality textbooks at a lower price.

3. Thirdly, make sure to take advantage of all sales. There is also a fantastic opportunity for students to take advantage of savings. Make sure to get your hands on it because some places or shops can offer you discounts.

CHAPTER 13

PRACTICE SELF-COMPASSION

What is self-compassion?

You must have a clear understanding of what self-compassion is and what it is not before we can discuss the ways in which self-compassion might be of assistance to you. In this chapter, I will tell you about how self-compassion can change your life. According to my observations, the term is frequently used as a synonym for several other notions that are related but unique, such as self-love and self-acceptance. Self-love and acceptance of one's identity are very healthy states of being. On the other hand, these characteristics are distinct from self-compassion in that they are based on the concept of the individual, which is distinct from other people. Self-compassion, on the other hand, necessitates acknowledging and enhancing our relationship with ourselves.

Most of us were not trained to recognize the universality of our experiences or to remind ourselves on a consistent basis that our happiness and our sadness are what tie us to all of humankind. Without a doubt, we were not! We were informed that we are "special" and "unique" and that we, as individuals, could make our own lives better and find solutions to our own problems. Is there a way to make a difficult day better? What steps can you take to achieve your professional objectives? Self-compassion of oneself!

In contrast to self-compassion, which takes a step back to examine both the individual and their position within the greater community, self-love is focused on the individual. There is yet another essential aspect to keep in mind. The thing that many of us were taught about self-compassion was that it was not always kind and tender, and it was not always tolerant of mistakes. The idea that an excessive amount of love will cause us to become complacent, lazy, and arrogant has almost always been a factor that has tempered the drive to cherish ourselves.

We make sure to have high expectations for ourselves and be attentive for any indication that we might be "going soft" to prevent ourselves from falling backward. If you want to be successful in your life and battle against procrastination, you need to pull just as powerfully in the opposite way. It is because it seems as though all the negative human qualities are continuously dragging us toward lethargy and mediocrity.

How does a student's lack of self-compassion contribute to their procrastination?

Self-compassion, which may be defined as the act of treating oneself with love and understanding in the face of failure or adversity, is an essential component in the process of developing educational achievement and overall well-being among students. As a student, you could be subjected to a wide variety of academic challenges, which might range from the stress of tests to the pressure of demanding schoolwork. You can experience negative impacts on your mental health if you are constantly striving for perfection. You may be being overly critical of yourself when you are confronted with a failure. Failure can lead to you being so critical of yourself that you may not be able to accept who you are as a person once you have experienced it. On the other side, the rigorous nature of your academic life can take a lead on your mental health. It can make you stress. It can contribute to your anxiety and even depression. This effect can be detrimental to your mental health. The manifestation of your lack of self-compassion can take the form of negative self-talk, in which you feel the need to criticize yourself for falling short of your own expectations. Individuals who are lacking in self-compassion may also suffer a decrease in their level of motivation. You are supposed to be able to experience joy and satisfaction in your academic endeavors. Yet, the fear of failing and harsh self-criticism that is connected with a lack of self-compassion are stealing those feelings away from you.

What kind of self-compassion one ought to have for oneself?

All of these things can make you more likely to procrastinate, and how you deal with them is entirely up to you. Find a way to overcome these challenges by cultivating self-compassion. It is normal to make mistakes; after all, you are only human. It is common for humans to make errors. Facing failure is possible. Take pleasure in your journey. The outcome is irrelevant. I am fine with you trying again. Be a little more forgiving with yourself as you learn to accept your journey, yourself, and your mistakes. You will find it easier to practice self-compassion in this manner. Being self-loving is crucial if you want to achieve success in life. It is clear that you need to put in some work, but it does not imply you should be too hard on yourself—practice self- and other compassion. Be easy on yourself, and everything will be fine.

Advantages of practicing self-compassion to combat procrastination:

1. An effective remedy for the paradox of procrastination is self-compassion. Overcoming procrastination and negative self-talk is possible when you treat yourself with compassion, empathy, and an awareness of your shared humanity.

2. You can overcome procrastination by practicing self-compassion, which can reawaken your natural motivation. When students are gentle with themselves, they are more likely to do things just because they enjoy them. Lessening of anxiety and outside influences is on the horizon.

3. You will be better able to handle stress and overcome obstacles if you can approach them with a loving perspective. When you do this, you will find that your stress and anxiety levels drop, which in turn makes you more productive and less likely to put things off till later.

4. Having compassion for yourself can assist you in being persistent with yourself, which will, in turn, assist you in working more effectively on yourself. It will be your assistance in overcoming procrastination.

5. Compassion for yourself is intimately connected to one's overall health and happiness. By treating yourself with the same level of love and compassion that you would offer to a friend, you are laying the groundwork for a constructive and caring relationship with yourself, which can be of assistance to you in the fight against procrastination.

CHAPTER 14

SELF-MONITORING

After talking about self-compassion, let's talk about your self-monitoring.

Let us say you had the intention of spending the few hours you had at home studying for the next test or tests you have scheduled. On the other hand, as you settle down to work on it, your phone continues to ring with notifications from the active social media scene. You began using your phone to engage in activities such as playing games, viewing videos on YouTube, or playing games that you enjoy the most. You may have decided to go out with your numerous buddies. It is due to the fact that you do not possess sufficient inhibitory control. As a result of your lack of, you are unable to refrain from checking your phone and chatting with your friends or on social media, and as a result, you wind up putting off the research assignment that you had planned to do. Because you do not have sufficient inhibitory control, it is possible that this is one of the primary reasons why you are procrastinating. There are things that you are unable to resist, which can lead to you putting things off. The use of self-monitoring is one of the most effective ways to deal with it.

What is self-monitoring?

Being able to keep tabs on your actions and how they impact you and those around you is what we mean when we talk about self-monitoring. Regarding you as a student, the act of observing and controlling your own actions, ideas, and performance within the context of academics is what is meant by the term "self-monitoring." It is a proactive approach to self-awareness and self-regulation, in which you actively track and assess many elements of your learning experiences. This will be an effective method for many students. Students are given the ability to make decisions based on accurate information, to establish attainable objectives, and to take responsibility for their academic achievement when they engage in this practice.

What are the impacts of inadequate self-monitoring on students?

A person with this level of social or interpersonal awareness is aware of both their own behavior and the reasons for other people's reactions to them. If you are impaired, it could be hard to tell when you are making progress or when you are falling behind, and you might always wonder why people act the way they do. Thus, a profound loss of self-awareness is an inevitable consequence of poor self-monitoring. Because of this, you may unconsciously allow your brain to control your thoughts and actions. You are more prone to damaging thought patterns and undesirable habits, such as procrastination, when you lack self-awareness and the capacity to think about your thoughts.

Students who struggle with inadequate self-monitoring tend to procrastinate. If you do not pay attention to your actions, you might not even notice that you are putting things off till later. Also, you will be less likely to feel the need to follow through on your promises and more likely to put things off till later if you do not know how your actions affect other people and yourself. You will procrastinate and be unable to take action to fix the problem if you do not self-monitor as a student.

As an example, let's say you have some tests coming up, and you are all prepared to study one day. But you find yourself engrossed in a discussion with your mom about various topics, and you never get down to the business at hand. Keeping the conversation going is perfectly OK in your eyes because it is directly related to your tests. You seem oblivious to the fact that you are being prevented from carrying out the task at hand because you are engaged in this very discussion. Unbeknownst to you, you are putting things off until later.

How might self-monitoring be adapted so that students can reap its benefits?

1. Identifying and addressing your procrastinating habits is made easier for you as a student when you engage in self-monitoring. You can avoid the detrimental effects that procrastination has on your academic duties by establishing deadlines, breaking down activities into smaller pieces, and reviewing your progress on a regular basis.

2. Students can manage to keep track of and divide up their time among many pursuits, such as academics, extracurriculars, and personal time. They will be able to manage their time better, find patterns, and improve their calendars with this.

3. On a frequent basis, students can evaluate how well they are doing in relation to their personal and educational goals. By utilizing self-monitoring approaches, you can break down larger goals into smaller, more achievable tasks. This way, you can measure your achievements and make improvements to your strategies as needed.

4. As a student, you can take an active part in assessing your own academic progress by keeping tabs on your test results, grades, and assignment comments. By doing so, they will be able to assess their strengths and weaknesses, which will allow them to adjust their study methods and get aid when they need it.

5. During your academic journey, you can find hurdles or obstacles by analyzing your own progress through self-monitoring. You are, therefore, in a position to establish proactive solutions, which may include obtaining further assistance, modifying your study strategies, or addressing personal aspects that may have an impact on your performance.

6. Students have the ability to monitor the things that can contribute to their stress and evaluate the coping techniques that they employ. Maintaining a balanced workload, using stress-reduction measures, and seeking support when necessary are all possible outcomes that can be accomplished by becoming aware of potential sources of stress.

7. It is possible to evaluate the development of fundamental abilities such as critical thinking, problem-solving, time management, and effective communication through the use of self-monitoring. In the process of cultivating individuals who are well-rounded and adaptive, this technique will contribute to your success.

8. Information on your decision-making processes can be obtained through the use of data collected through self-monitoring. Suppose you have a comprehensive grasp of

your capabilities, preferences, and areas in which you could develop. In that case, you will be able to make educated judgments regarding the courses you take, the extracurricular activities you participate in, and the potential professional options you pursue.

CHAPTER 15

GROWTH MINDSET

A brief introduction to the concept of a growth mindset was provided in the previous chapters. Let's go into more depth about it now, shall we?

A conflict between two mentalities, namely the Fixed and the Growth mindsets:

First, we need to understand the mindsets that people normally have. People can be divided into two distinct mentalities. One is a fixed attitude, while the other is a growing mindset. Let's talk about it in a little more detail so we can discern between it. When a person has a fixed mindset, they tend to assume that people are born with a predetermined level of intelligence, skill, and potential. Those with a fixed mindset frequently put forth a lot of effort to avoid failing or appearing foolish when confronted with difficult circumstances. As a result, they deprive themselves of the opportunity to gain valuable life experiences.

On the other hand, people with a growth mindset generally believe they have the capacity to learn and develop in any field if they put in the necessary amount of effort, perseverance, and practice. Intelligence, ability, and talent are all things that may be cultivated under this attitude, provided that one is willing to put in the effort to do so. Fixed mindsets are, without a shadow of a doubt, less attractive than development mindsets in the context of the discussion on which mindset is superior. This is due to the restricted space that fixed mindsets have. People with a growth mindset are more likely to take on challenges and accept that learning from their mistakes and overcoming hurdles are essential components of personal development. We believe that it is essential to have a clear understanding of which of the two mindsets—growth or fixed—is the one that you tend to have the most. Begin by considering whether you have a fixed mindset or a growing attitude. Let us imagine that after giving it some thought, you have the impression that you have a fixed mindset. However, at this point in your life, when you have a hard time overcoming your tendency to put things off procrastinating, don't you think that you could be interested in adopting a growth mindset in order to gain a deeper comprehension, make changes in your routines, and have a more promising future?

The idea of having a growth mindset.

To put it simply, the concept of a fixed mindset vs a growing mindset is a psychological one. Carol Dweck, a psychologist, is the one who came up with the idea of a growth mindset, which is a psychological concept that expresses the view that one's abilities and intelligence can be increased through dedication, hard effort, learning, and resilience. Through the process of molding their attitudes and behaviors toward learning and obstacles, students can be assisted in overcoming procrastination through the utilization of a growth mindset. Fear of failure, beliefs that are rooted in a fixed mindset, or a lack of drive are frequently the root causes of procrastination. With the cultivation of a growth mindset, these problems may be addressed, and students will be equipped with the attitude and tools necessary to approach activities more efficiently.

How is it achievable for a student to have a growth mentality for his future?

Achieve a deeper level of understanding.

Before you can begin to cultivate a development mindset, the first thing you need to do is comprehend the concept itself. It is important for you to be aware that intelligence and abilities are not permanent characteristics but rather things that may be developed over time via devotion and constant effort. Gaining an overview of the research on growth mindsets and fixed mindsets can offer you a foundational understanding of the topic.

Gaining wisdom from your past mistakes.

When you have a growth mindset, you view your failures and losses not as indications of your own limitations but rather as useful lessons that contribute to your personal development and growth toward improvement. I am requesting that you be encouraged to think about the blunders you have made, to comprehend the elements that contributed to your failure, and to devise methods for reaching your goals of growth.

Seize both opportunities and challenges.

A person with a growth mentality should see setbacks not as impossible problems but as chances to grow and develop. You may reframe adversities as inevitable parts of learning if you encourage yourself to have a positive attitude toward them. Important roles can be played by parents, mentors, and educators who stress the need to confront problems directly as a means to one's intellectual and personal development.

Practicing self-love.

What you say to yourself has a significant influence on your state of mind. It would be wise for you to practice encouraging good self-talk. One must replace negative self-beliefs with positive self-affirmations that support the idea that one can grow and improve. If you find yourself telling yourself things like "I can't do this," try rephrasing it as "I can't do this yet."

Rejoice in your progress.

Rather than being fixated on the goal alone, it is important to celebrate your trip. The best tip for developing a growth mindset is to enjoy the process of learning as much as you enjoy the destination itself. When adopting a growth mindset, it is important to place more emphasis on the process of learning as opposed to merely focusing on the outcome. You should be sure to give yourself praise and encouragement for the amount of work, time, effort, persistence, and techniques that you have utilized along the learning journey, regardless of the end that you have achieved. You should celebrate not only the accomplishment but also all you have accomplished along the way.

CHAPTER 16

ACCEPTANCE OF CONSTRUCTIVE CRITICISM

The human communication process includes an intriguing component known as Criticism. There are many ways in which its interaction contributes to the formation of people's perspectives. It is something that has the potential to encourage progress and to affect the norms of society.

Criticism spans a spectrum of expressions that range from helpful input to more scathing statements despite the fact that it is frequently seen with a negative connotation. As a general rule and a broad definition, Criticism is the act of evaluating, analyzing, and providing feedback on someone or something or on oneself. Criticism can also refer to the act of providing feedback on your own self. Involved in this process is the expressing of opinions, judgments, or assessments that are based on personal standards, societal norms, or professional criteria.

What different kinds of Criticism are there?

Criticism can be broken down into several categories. There are many different kinds of Criticism, such as constructive feedback that is targeted at improvement, academic Criticism, literary reviews, and even destructive Criticism. Critical feedback that is damaging and has the potential to cause harm or destroy confidence is the most dangerous type.

What is the nature of Criticism?

Criticism is essentially subjective, reflecting the many perspectives and values that people hold. This is the nature of Criticism. Different people may have different reactions to the same circumstance or piece of art, which might result in a wide range of opinions and criticisms. Personal experiences, cultural backgrounds, and individual tastes are frequently the starting points for Criticism, which is characterized by its subjective nature.

Criticism for students at the academic level.

The influence that Criticism has on students is significant. Your feelings, your self-esteem, and your motivation can all be affected by it, which might have repercussions for your future. Feedback that is both positive and constructive might motivate you to make progress in your development. The development of resilience and a sense of accomplishment will be facilitated as a result of this.

The flip side of Criticism is known as negative Criticism, and it is the opposite of positive Criticism. The impact it has on your academic performance can be tremendous.

You may have feelings of self-doubt, demoralization, and even avoidance of future activities as a result of receiving harsh feedback.

Recognize, however, that the emotional impact of Criticism frequently depends on the circumstances in which it is delivered. Additionally, it may be contingent upon the nature of the relationship that exists between the critic and the recipient, as well as the manner in which the feedback is conveyed. Providing students with well-articulated and constructive feedback in academic contexts can lead to advancements in both their academic and professional careers. Critiques that are harsh or unfair, on the other hand, may impede their personal and professional development, generating obstacles that stand in the way of their achievement.

Criticism and Its Positive Impact on You as a Student.

Encouraging your own development.

Students' personal development is greatly aided by constructive Criticism, which is essential, yet receiving harsh Criticism can be emotionally taxing. Your progress will be accelerated by it. You will gain useful insights and be able to identify problem areas with its support. Constructive Criticism, when taken in stride and with an open mind, can help you become more self-aware and improve your abilities, leading to your overall personal development.

Make room for your improvement.

Critical feedback might prompt you to examine your choices, outputs, and performance. The best way to figure out where you are academically and how others see you is to ask around. Your battle against procrastination will be built upon this self-awareness.

Strengthen your endurance.

You may strengthen your resilience by learning to take criticism constructively. You can overcome obstacles by cultivating resilience. It is crucial to see Criticism as a chance for improvement, keep a cheerful attitude in the face of adversity, and resist the urge to put things off till later.

Enhance your communication abilities.

Taking part in the exchange of helpful Criticism will help you hone your communication abilities. Mastering the art of effective argumentation is within your reach. Pay close attention, and then answer with care. Your ability to communicate with others, whether in a professional or academic context, will improve as a result.

Encourage yourself to engage in constructive self-criticism.

There are instances when students are so critical of themselves that they begin to view everything in a negative light instead. They become so critical of themselves that it constitutes a barrier that stands in the way of their achievement of accomplishment. Always take the time to provide constructive feedback to yourself. Constructive Criticism of oneself has the potential to become an effective instrument for one's own personal development and improvement. Self-criticism can become a tool for self-improvement, better self-awareness, and overall well-being if it is done with a constructive perspective. You will be able to overcome your negative habits and your tendency to put things off. The act of actively recognizing and celebrating your accomplishments and talents is accomplished through the practice of positive self-criticism.

Recognizing your own skills can be beneficial to your self-esteem and can serve as a basis for establishing and accomplishing your long-term objectives.

It has the potential to cultivate a growth mentality in which difficulties are seen as opportunities for personal development and knowledge acquisition. Therefore, try not to be too hard on yourself. Your missteps should not be viewed as failures; rather, you should view them as stepping stones on the path to your personal and professional progress. It is acceptable to have a more tolerant and optimistic attitude toward yourself because it will help you have a better future.

CHAPTER 17

MEDITATION: HEALTH IS ALSO IMPORTANT

When people think of "meditation," they might picture a group of monks seated cross-legged in a temple, their eyes closed while they chant mantras. But these days, anyone with a little amount of information and skill can practice meditation; it is no longer limited to monks or those who have studied the discipline for years.

What is meditation?

Meditation has a wide variety of practices that help one become more aware of their internal experiences, more attuned to their immediate surroundings, or just more relaxed and at peace with themselves.

Meditation can be as simple as taking a few deep breaths or as involved as going for a stroll in the park. Words like "unknown" and "mysterious" can also be connected to the meaning of meditation. Thinking, pondering, or contemplating is the meaning of the Latin term "meditato," from which the English word "meditation" is derived. Being able to meditate allows us to temporarily quiet our racing thoughts while keeping our bodies and brains fully present. At first, the idea could appear complicated; nevertheless, after you put it into practice, you will discover how easy it is.

What role does meditation have in the prevention of procrastination among students?

The practice of meditation has the potential to contribute significantly to the success of students in overcoming procrastination and improving their overall academic performance.

» Students frequently engage in procrastination as a result of the tension and anxiety they have around the completion of their work and assignments. It can give you a reduction in stress, which can be beneficial for them. Students can also benefit from it by gaining the ability to manage better and alleviate the pressure that is associated with their academic duties and deadlines.

» A mind that is composed is less likely to engage in procrastination. It can assist you in managing your feelings by cultivating an awareness of your feelings that is free from judgment. Reducing the emotional barriers that contribute to procrastination is one of the benefits of developing emotional resilience.

» Similarly, a growth mindset, which is the concept that one's capabilities may be developed through effort and perseverance, can be encouraged by the practice of meditation. Students who have a growth mindset are more inclined to embrace problems without the fear of failing, which, in turn, reduces the urge to procrastinate.

» Fostering a non-judgmental awareness of their sentiments will assist you in regulating your own emotions, which will help you better manage your own feelings. Meditation can help you feel more connected to your beliefs and goals, which can enhance your overall intrinsic drive.

» During your time as a student, you will cultivate a more distinct sense of purpose and motivation. Your propensity to put things off till later will decrease as a result of your increased ability to take the initiative and tackle duties in a timely manner.

» Lack of sleep and erratic sleep patterns are two factors that might make procrastination more difficult to manage. Through the encouragement of relaxation and the reduction of insomnia, meditation has been demonstrated to improve the quality of sleep. Getting enough sleep and rest is essential for students in order for them to fulfill their goals. A sufficient amount of restful sleep will improve your cognitive function and decision-making abilities, which in turn can reduce the likelihood that you will engage in procrastination.

» A positive mindset can be fostered through the practice of meditation by cultivating feelings of gratitude, self-compassion, and a sense of well-being inside oneself. It is more probable that you will tackle issues with optimism if you have a positive mindset when you are confronted with them. The likelihood of procrastination brought on by pessimism or bad emotions will be reduced as a result of this move.

» Frequently, negative thought patterns, such as self-criticism or skepticism, are the root cause of procrastination by individuals. Through meditation, you can develop a more sympathetic and positive mindset, which will make it easier to absorb these thoughts without criticizing them. By making this mental change, you can disrupt the cycle of negative ideas that contribute to your tendency to put things off until later.

Approaches a student can adapt for Mediation.

There are a variety of approaches that a student can take to meditate in order to combat procrastination; however, before proceeding, it is important to note that exercising mindfulness and practicing meditation are two distinct components. Students can become more conscious via the practice of mindfulness, and practicing mindfulness will also help them meditate and concentrate more effectively. Although there is a connection between them, and they do go together, they are two distinct disciplines.

Different ways that students can practice meditation.

1. First, I really recommend guided meditations, particularly for those who are just beginning. Whether you are looking to relax, reduce stress, or practice mindfulness, you can find a guided meditation session on any number of websites or applications.

2. A more manageable approach could be to begin with shorter periods of meditation. At first, aim for 5 to 10 minutes, and then, as you get more comfortable and experienced, you can prolong the period.

3. Settle into a cozy spot where you won't be interrupted unless absolutely necessary. A secluded spot in a room, a park, or even a library could fit the bill. This will assist you in maintaining concentration.

4. Then, take a seat or lie down wherever you feel most at ease. As you sit down, make sure your back is straight and put your hands on your lap or knees. If you want to lie

down, make sure you have a sturdy surface to rest your head and arms on.

5. To reduce the amount of outside noise, close your eyes.

6. Direct your focus on your breathing. Take note of the pulsation of your chest and belly as you inhale and exhale or the natural cadence of your breath.

7. Here and now, pay attention. Ideas can just pop into your head. Instead of trying to push them away, just be aware that they are there, judgment-free. Then, slowly return your attention to your breathing.

8. Learning to meditate is a process that takes practice. If you find that your thoughts wander while practicing, try not to feel too down on yourself.

Find out what works best for you by trying out various meditation techniques. Some examples of such practices are walking meditation, body scan meditation, loving-kindness meditation, and mindfulness meditation.

CHAPTER 18

PAY ATTENTION TO YOUR MENTAL HEALTH

It has been a long journey up to this point, but we have now arrived at what may be the most significant component of the fight against procrastination. It is the element that determines whether or not one will have a happy future or a miserable one in the future. Your outlook and the way you are on the inside could be altered as a result. It has the potential to change your aspirations and goals, and it can either strengthen you or break your heart. It is, without a doubt, something that requires a great deal of care. At this point in your life, it is the most influential factor.

Your mental and emotional health is important.

This factor refers to the status of your mental and emotional wellness at the moment. You must maintain your mental health in order to remain strong, and your struggle against procrastination and your mental condition can have an immediate impact on everything, or even worse, in a couple of seconds. Maintaining control over these two areas may demand the greatest effort out of everything else that needs to be maintained. It is going to take your utmost concentration. Negativity has the potential to take control of your mental state, and depression can become a significant problem if you do not take the necessary precautions to mitigate its effects. It could take you years to have a bright future or to be conscious of what is going on within yourself and your life if you cannot feel at peace and if you cannot think positively. Depression and anxiety are both conditions that can be challenging to manage; nevertheless, they are both manageable, and there are other options available to manage these concerns. Taking into consideration the state of mind in general, the mind needs to be cared for continuously and maintained on a regular basis. As a teenager, you may have difficulty establishing a connection with yourself that is of an undeniably healthy kind. Although it is frequently the most difficult thing you will ever have to do in your lifetime, it is also possible that it will be the best thing you can accomplish in your entire life. Providing that you are able to successfully organize your thoughts, there is nothing that you are unable to accomplish.

The ways in which students can keep their mental health in check.

Your mental health maintenance should be a priority for you as a student because it has the potential to determine the course of your future. Tackling the issue of procrastination is an important component of this effort. Students can learn to protect their mental health and combat procrastination by employing the following tactics, which are practical in nature:

Say by to negative thinking.

The first step is to stop thinking negatively, so keep that in mind. The belief that "I don't have enough" is prevalent among people who struggle with poor self-esteem, anxiety, despair, or both. This claim lacks validity. It is as far from reality as it gets, in fact. It is a tool of negativity that our brains make up to prevent us from being happy or even reaching our maximum potential. Keep in mind that just because it occurs does not indicate that you are flawed. Consequently, do your best to dispel those ideas and remind yourself that you are, and always have been, more than enough to accomplish your goals.

Find the roots.

Find out what is really going on with your academics and why you are feeling down and anxious. Figure out why you procrastinate. It can be due to anxiety over making a mistake, an obsession with perfection, a lack of drive, or something else entirely. Try to get to the bottom of things. It will be useful for guiding the creation of focused plans for enhancement.

Just let it out.

Make yourself believe that you are having a feeling. It will be impossible to foresee every possible outcome. Sometimes, you may find it difficult to maintain your mental concentration. Those days when you cannot seem to conjure a single thought. Mornings when you feel down and out. Just let yourself feel the agony or despair for a while. When you succeed, stand tall and proud. Try your best, even though it's not always easy. Dealing with your negative emotions will become easier for you.

Take self-care as your priority.

Begin Making time for self-care a top priority. Get enough rest, work out frequently, and eat well. Mental health and resistance to procrastination's harmful consequences are both enhanced when the body is well-nourished and gets enough sleep.

Being optimistic.

Get going, Aiming for the bright side. Permit yourself to be happy and optimistic. Take a moment to reflect on what brings you joy and what you would like to accomplish. The only thing you really need is the will to improve yourself. Stopping for a second to tell yourself that you are doing better than what you are going through can be all it takes. Things are looking up for you now.

Have realistic expectations.

It is possible that your unrealistic expectations influence your thinking. Make sure your expectations are reasonable. Your mental stability will improve. As a major factor, perfectionism might cause people to put things off until later. Accepting that being human means making errors and accepting that you will never be perfect.

It is okay to ask for help.

You could use some help. No matter what, get in touch with someone. It might be a family member or a friend. Perhaps it will be more useful to you than you realize. Open it up to them about how you are feeling, and they will see a side of you that you might have missed. Talk to them and be honest; they might reciprocate, and you might find that you reveal more than you thought. Keep in mind that nothing is more important than your emotional health. Seeking assistance is a suitable course of action. Do not hesitate to seek assistance if you believe you need it. Getting help is never a disgrace. On the contrary, admitting you need help shows bravery and strength. I do not see any problem with this.

Appreciate your accomplishments.

No matter how minor, it is important to recognize and appreciate your accomplishments. As a result of the positive reinforcement it provides, you will feel more motivated and accomplished, and procrastination will be less likely to take root.

CHAPTER 19

MOTIVATION THROUGH REWARD SCHEMES

In this chapter, I will go over why it is so crucial to keep yourself motivated while you are trying to overcome procrastination.

Role of motivations against procrastination

Instead of actively seeking to create drive inside themselves, most youngsters wait for it to happen. You may have been sitting around for quite some time, hoping that inspiration will hit. Whenever it hit, I would have a brief period of intense motivation, but it would always go just as quickly.

Think about it ' when I experience these intense spurts of motivation, what is it that drives me? 'Given your ability to answer this question, it was only natural that you would also possess the ability to reproduce the effect. At long last, the response arrived. Having the ability to stay motivated, capable of making some truly remarkable changes to your life.

We should go into more depth on the idea of motivation. Where does the word "motivation" come from? THE DRIVE. You may have chosen to take action after experiencing several ups and downs, but now you want to change the pattern of failure, and that is why you are here. In order to remain driven, we must possess an irresistible incentive that propels us toward our desired destination. The question "WHY do I even want to do this?" must be at the forefront of our minds at all times. If the answer to that question does not compel you, then either reevaluate your motivations or alter your objective entirely.

Importance of motivation for students.

On my path, I realized that anytime I felt incredibly driven and inspired to make a difference, it was because I was envisioning my ideal future self. All the reasons I had for doing this were running through my head. Why would I bother to get out of bed and work if those weren't the case? Without ambition and a plan for the future, I would merely exist as a lazy couch potato. Most people never change their lives because they are afraid to dream big. Students can achieve their dreams with the help of their inspiring motivation. Staying motivated can help them in achieving the whole world. Motivating yourself and reaching your full potential requires insight into the thoughts and feelings of those who have already achieved great achievements.

A student's ability to take initiative, stay focused on their objectives, and overcome obstacles depends on their level of motivation, which is a mental state. If students are motivated, they are more likely to be actively involved in their education, have a genuine interest in and love of learning, and achieve better results in the classroom. But with such a wide variety of interests, personalities, and learning styles represented in any given classroom, inspiring pupils can be no easy feat.

The Importance of Incentive Programs for Inspiration.

Students can stay motivated to attain their goals and the future they desire for themselves by rewarding themselves for every little and great achievement. These are the plans that can assist you in reaching your goals by rewarding yourself for each achievement.

Using rewards and public praise for good conduct, academic success, or other goals, reward systems provide a systematic way to motivate pupils. Aligning student objectives with the rewards they get, these schemes tap into both inner and extrinsic motivation. Some of the ways in which incentive programs boost motivation are as follows:

1. As a student, you will be motivated to establish attainable objectives, and when you reach them, you will be rewarded accordingly.

2. Your combination of intrinsic and extrinsic motivation can be achieved through well-designed reward systems. In contrast to extrinsic motivation, which is based on things like accolades, material incentives, or personal fulfillment, intrinsic motivation is based on things like the love of learning and the happiness that comes from within. You manage to find a happy medium between these two forms of incentive in your successful reward systems. In contrast to extrinsic motivation, which is based on things like accolades, material incentives, or personal fulfillment, intrinsic motivation is based on things like the love of learning and the happiness that comes from within.

3. Students who are inspired to succeed do better academically. Students are captivated and encouraged to actively participate in a stimulating and engaging learning environment that is created via the use of reward programs.

4. Motive flourishes in an encouraging classroom setting. By highlighting accomplishments, giving credit where credit

is due, and encouraging a more success-oriented culture, rewarding schemes help bring about this kind of atmosphere.

5. Students develop a sense of competence when they achieve achievement through rewarding methods. Students gain self-assurance and the conviction that they can conquer obstacles when they receive praise and acknowledgment for their efforts.

CHAPTER 20

POSITIVE AFFIRMATIONS ARE THE KEY

Now let's talk about your own self. I have awful news for you. Yes, we are going to start with the bad news. You are not fully prepared to change yourself. It is primarily because identifying the issue is necessary before attempting to resolve it. And now for the ride. Perhaps you've given up hope. You no longer believe in yourself. You have lost hope for the future because of your bad habits and procrastination, which keep you far from achieving your goals. You have lost faith in turning things around and finding your way back. At this point, you may think that no one—not even your parents, teachers, or peers—can assist you in putting things right.

First, evaluate within yourself if you are prepared to make changes in your life in order to have a better future. You may receive a response within yourself indicating that you can continue with these practices and that you can no longer put your future at risk.

Now, the task is to determine how to restore your hope. We both understand how difficult that will be. Most likely, you are unlikely less prepared yet to work on it. However, we also know that you are willing to change, not because you care about anyone else but yourself. Fundamentally, you're a person who firmly believes that you have the ability to change and that you will undoubtedly do so. You're actually prepared to commit your entire life to helping yourselves grow into your greatest selves. We both know that you're looking for a change at this time in your life. You are here to help you obtain what you want, but it can be difficult and simple to become overwhelmed by things, causing you to put things off, delay, or procrastinate. You are the only one here. It is your responsibility to assist yourself in rediscovering hope if you claim to have lost it. You are the only one who can accomplish it if anyone can!

Have faith in yourself.

It is a terrible strategy to solve problems if you do not believe in yourself. Before thinking about seeking a solution, believe in yourself and know you can change.

Here is an example from a story you loved when you were a kid to help illustrate the point. Do you recall the story of the pitcher and the crow? Where an emaciated crow had exhausted all possible sources of water. Things were looking bleak. The crow eventually found a pitcher of water. Her requests were granted. Unfortunately, the crow could not dip her beak into the bottom of the pitcher to get a drink, and there was hardly enough water to go around when she peered inside. So, she began to fill the pitcher with stones one by one, and eventually, the water began to rise gently.

At last, the water level was just right for the crow to sip from, providing a refreshing drink of water. No matter how bad things seem at the moment, there's always room for improvement. There is always a chance. Act like a crow. Day after day, you will see yourself climbing the ladder to your best future as you drop stones of empathy, understanding, compassion, and bravery into your classroom.

Use the power of Self Affirmations

Positive or negative affirmations are only suggestions and thoughts you offer yourself. You can influence your mental attitude by feeding your subconscious mind recommendations as you make them to yourself.

Instilling a good or optimistic outlook on life is as simple as giving constructive ideas and recommendations to your subconscious mind. Because your subconscious mind cannot tell the difference between truth and fantasy, it will begin to accept your positive, encouraging thoughts as fact the more you bombard them. Imagine progress, fresh ideas, and growth. This outlook will give you the confidence to chase your dreams and believe in yourself. On top of that, good things will come your way when you think positively.

If you want to change, you can. Just tell yourself that. Say these repeatedly to inspire yourself to overcome procrastination and create a brighter future for yourself and those you will meet. You need to remind yourself of these affirmations constantly.

1. It is for "ME, MYSELF, AND I" that I am making this effort.

2. I can overcome my vices and achieve my goals for the future.

3. I am in charge, and I get to decide what happens next.

4. By accepting myself as I am and learning to change for the better, I can find happiness no matter what challenges life throws at me.

5. I am gaining the ability to be patient with myself, accept my imperfections, forgive myself, and keep moving towards what I want and deserve.

6. I can forgive myself for my faults since they were only the universe's way of directing me to all I desire; at my core, I am pure and innocent.

7. Every day, I move closer to my goals, and it feels great just to know that I am getting closer.

8. Things are moving along according to plan. Everything I have ever dreamed of being is about to come true for me.

9. I consider it done if I am contemplating altering my identity.

10. The lessons of the past have prepared me well for the future, and I am ready to put them behind me and concentrate on what is ahead.

11. Right now, I can be whoever I want since I am no longer bound by the identity I formerly believed to be true to myself.

12. I can intentionally eliminate the concepts and mental programs that have shaped my personality and create a fresh route toward great things. Even though I was unaware of adopting these programs, I can now choose to do so.

13. I am starting to reassert my control and authority over my life, which has always been within me.

14. By concentrating on my desires, I can start making them a reality.

15. Using my power to construct my experience through my ideas and intentions, life is getting more and more thrilling.

16. I am thankful for today because it is only one more chance to feel the happiness of reaching my full potential.

17. Just being myself and being myself is all that's required of me—no need to make a difference or gain fame or popularity.

CHAPTER 21

PUT MINDFULNESS INTO PRACTICE

A student's conscience performs an essential role in their lives. It is possible to argue that spending time improving your memory can yield the greatest "study bang" for your time if you use it wisely. There may be instances where a student begins to avoid things that require too much mental effort because they lack the necessary mental capacity. It leads them toward procrastination. They will start avoiding, contributing to their bad habits. Remember that it does not matter how quickly you go through your textbooks if you cannot even recall the material you studied five minutes later. Organizing yourself is important, but only if you do not miss quizzes or forget to turn in homework. Of course, it is not the best way to start the study day by spending hours looking for necessities like your phone, glasses, keys, and other items. Even in study skills courses, basic memory procedures are the study ingredients that are least likely to be taught in schools despite their importance. Therefore, many educational institutions and instructors may assist you with organizing, writing, reading, and test-taking techniques. However, far too many of them will still "forget" to assist you with memory and consciousness.

Having mind consciousness is also crucial for mental maximization. The term "mind consciousness" refers to focused attention or mindfulness. It is an advantageous mindset that can greatly improve the caliber of your academic work. Being mindful is focusing all of one's attention on the here and now, avoiding being sidetracked by ideas about the past or future. By incorporating mindfulness into your studies, you can increase concentration, enhance memory retention, lessen stress, and have a more successful learning experience overall.

Why do you lack mental focus?

Our bodies have three components that aid in memory.

- » Retention
- » Remember
- » Recognition

You can use these aspects of memory development to address the reasons behind your forgetfulness as you consider them. Examine the information below and consider whether you are engaging in activities that enhance your learning ability. One of these regions is typically the source of memory problems:

1. You are unable to give the information any meaning.
2. You did not study the necessary information.
3. You do not understand what needs to be kept in mind.
4. You are not motivated to recall.
5. You let boredom or apathy control how we learn.
6. You do not have a specific learning habit.
7. You use our study time in an unorganized and ineffective manner.
8. You do not apply the understanding we have acquired.

Methods that can help you boost your learning capacity.

These are some ways that you can use to increase your mental capacity for learning.

Decide to remember.

What you consciously choose to remember is what you remember. If you don't want to recall a certain piece of knowledge or don't believe you can do so, then you won't remember it! The content must be something you want to remember, and you must be convinced that you will remember it for you to remember it.

Having an understanding in your unique way.

What you comprehend is the only thing that you will remember. When you read something and come away with an understanding of what it is trying to convey, you have started the process of retention. To rephrase the message using your own words is the action that you can take. Are you able to provide a concise summary of the primary concept?

You will not be able to select whether to recall or forget what is being stated until you completely comprehend what is being communicated to you.

Learning that goes above what is required of you.

You must go beyond merely completing your assignment to enhance the amount of mental adherence you have. Learning anything in-depth, sometimes known as "over-learning," is the best way to ensure you retain the information you acquire. A preliminary reading of the text is required for this. It is possible to perform a critical reading, and it is also possible to have some specific ways of reviewing that will reinforce what you ought to have learned before.

Becoming aware of the pattern.

You must first notice the pattern to understand why you continue to experience the same problem of forgetting things. Construct a pattern that will allow you to recall your lesson and concentrate on your studies most effectively. You should have a method that will assist you in remembering how the information is connected and organized. Attaching or associating what you are attempting to recall to something already present in your memory can be useful and efficient.

Engaging in mindful practices to combat mindlessness-related procrastination.

Practicing mindfulness regularly might help you lead a more balanced and fulfilling life as you can pursue your academic goals. These can help you, but try various approaches until you discover one that works for you.

1. A few minutes of focused breathing might help you begin or finish your day. Put focus on your breath as you inhale and exhale slowly. Relaxation and enhanced concentration are the results.

2. Make a conscious effort to start each day with a positive intention.

3. Be an attentive listener in class, whether you are leading a discussion or just chatting with your friends.

4. Consider your life's ups and downs, good and bad, without passing judgment.

5. Schedule times during the day when you will not use any electronic devices. If you want to be less distracted by

technology and more fully immersed in the here and now, try turning off your displays for a while.

6. Take part in mindful activities when you need a break from studying. A quick stroll, stretching, or a meditation session could all help clear your head.

7. Keep a gratitude notebook to help you appreciate the good things in your life. One way to maintain an optimistic outlook and lessen the effects of stress is to keep a gratitude journal.

CHAPTER 22

SEEKING ADVICE AND ASSISTANCE

In this chapter, I will tell you about Assistance. One effective tactic for students to fight procrastination is to ask for and accept assistance from others. When students are faced with a massive undertaking, they can find a way to tackle it step by step by obtaining assistance. They have knowledge and ideas that can help you tackle your problems in a different way. Students develop a sense of ownership over their work when they enlist the help of others, be it peers, teachers, or mentors. One way to keep yourself motivated is to let someone else know what you are aiming toward. Receiving assistance from a mentor can boost your confidence and ability, lowering the likelihood of procrastination, especially if a particular assignment needs skills that you are still developing as a student.

Getting assistance from your study group.

If you are looking for some study group assistance, I recommend inviting at least four other students, but at most six. The goal is to maximize the group's knowledge and expertise while giving every student an equal opportunity to participate.

Members of the group should not be inseparable, but they also should not be too friendly either. Encourage a range of perspectives and insist on shared commitment.

Pick pupils who are just as serious, dedicated, and intelligent as you are. That will give you a little push to keep going.

Receive guidance from your instructor.

It is important to carefully consider your teacher's personality type, including their likes, dislikes, preferences, teaching style, and

Anticipated outcomes. No matter the subject or format, the amount of time spent preparing for a lesson might vary greatly depending on your "profile" of the teachers involved.

As a student, you are advised to ask questions in class if you do not understand anything, so that is one option to think about. Teachers might vary greatly in their approach to student participation; some are comfortable answering questions at any point in the class, some would rather students wait until the end of the day's lecture, and yet others actively discourage student participation of any kind.

Get to know your professors' preferred methods of answering inquiries and ask them when and how they like it.

Many educators are afraid they will lose control if their classes stray too far from their carefully crafted lesson plans, regardless of how prepared their students are for an open-ended debate. Teachers with this attitude may try to spark class discussion, but they will always be looking for ways to direct the conversation toward their lesson plan. You can never tell what's going to happen in a classroom where some teachers thrive on chaos. In any event, they are still your instructor, and they will do their best to assist you in overcoming your procrastination and accomplishing what you want to accomplish. If you need assistance, feel free to ask them. Make an effort to classify your teacher's remarks as you listen to him. You can use this information to figure out how they can improve your study habits. A simple method to ask a lecturer for help without coming out as overly obedient is to remain after class on occasion or to drop by during their office hours.

Model your behavior after that of an exemplary person.

There are many areas of life that might benefit greatly from having an exemplary role model to look up to for encouragement, ideas, and direction. If you have someone to look up to—a mentor, a role model, or just someone who has your back—you will be more motivated to succeed in the future.

You might draw inspiration and drive from a role model. The accomplishments and character traits of an admired person might inspire you to strive for your own dreams and realize your ambitions.

When you have an admired figure in your life, you are more likely to have access to mentoring and advice. Insights, stories, and guidance from mentors can help you face issues head-on and make smart choices.

CHAPTER 23

TRACK YOUR PROGRESS

fter talking about Assistance, let's talk about tracking your progress.

What is tracking progress?

Monitoring, measuring, and evaluating one's own path toward goals or objectives is an essential part of the ever-changing process of tracking progress for students. As a tool for empowerment and growth, tracking progress is crucial in the area of education. Especially for teens, it is crucial. It is critical to keep tabs on what your progress comprises. In order to emphasize the many advantages of tracking progress, it is necessary to go into the particular significance of doing so as well as how students generally can do so. Data collecting, analysis of results, and plan revisions in light of new information are all parts of it. Whether you are aiming for career success, personal growth, or academic excellence, keeping tabs on your progress gives you honest feedback and shows you the way to get there.

Why monitoring progress is important?

Students gain a clear picture of their aims and aspirations when they keep track of their progress. It helps them track their development and find areas for improvement so they can reach their academic and personal goals. Additionally, it aids pupils in recognizing their own areas of strength and improvement. Being aware of one's strengths helps one to play to those strengths, while being aware of one's flaws allows one to work on those deficiencies specifically. It aids in maintaining their motivation. By keeping tabs on his progress, a student can zero in on his own growth. Students may learn a lot about how they manage their time by keeping track of their progress. They can figure out what they are doing that takes too much time and come up with plans to be more productive in school. However, by offering a systematic method for overcoming problems and disappointments, monitoring progress enables pupils to adjust to new situations.

Ways to Track your progress.

These are some of the strategies that might assist you in avoiding procrastination to the greatest extent possible.

1. Establish Your Objectives Clearly.

2. Make use of notebooks and calendars.

3. Build your own list of tasks.

4. Always keep a journal of your progress.

5. Organize your to-do list.

6. Apps that are based on technology should be used.

7. Regularly evaluate how well you are performing.

8. Request Feedback and Keep an Eye on Your Grades and Test Scores

9. Develop your own academic portfolios.

10. Conduct an Analysis of Time-Management Techniques

11. Maintain a careful watc

CHAPTER 24

ASSEMBLE YOUR FUTURE

The entirety of this chapter is devoted to your journey into the future. It is important to first consider whether you are prepared for the future. Can you say that you are completely ready for the future? The decisions you make today and the way you organize yourself for the future will determine the type of future you will have.

The greatest moment for you to start putting together your future is while you are in your teenage years. By focusing on your procrastination on both a personal and academic level, you will be able to reach the bright future you know you deserve. It is a wide and undiscovered territory that contains the promise of fresh chances, challenges, and your own personal development. The future belongs to you. It is of the utmost importance for students to comprehend the significance of the future and work actively toward influencing it. When you are in the stage of being a student, it is essential to have a clear understanding of why the future is significant for you, as well as how you may give yourself insights into how you can construct your future through proactive planning, the establishment of goals, and a dedication to learning throughout your entire life.

Why students should be concerned about their future?

It is crucial to consider your future for a number of different reasons. These are some of them:

1. In your capacity as a student, the future can serve as the basis upon which you construct your own personal and professional development. A canvas on which you can

paint your hopes, dreams, and objectives is represented by this metaphor.

2. The student's hope for the future serves as a source of inspiration for them. During the difficult times that you are going through, it will serve as a guiding light, providing you with a sense of hope and purpose. Students have the ability to develop resilience by visualizing a compelling future for themselves.

3. Having a vision of the future can provide you with the resources you need to make it through difficult situations. The ability to anticipate prospective obstacles enables proactive planning and the development of problem-solving skills, regardless of whether the obstacle involves academic, personal, or professional endeavors.

4. As a student, you have the opportunity to paint your sense of purpose onto the future on a canvas that serves as a canvas. The process of putting together your future will require you to integrate your own values, passions, and interests with your long-term objectives.

5. Being aware of the significance you hold for the future places the obligation of personal responsibility on your shoulders as a student. Students are able to comprehend that the decisions they make in the present have a direct influence on the future they will experience. This empowerment motivates people to make proactive decisions and to take responsibility for their actions. A commitment to ethical and responsible behavior is created as a result of this.

6. Students who have a comprehensive understanding of the significance of the future are better able to adjust to changing circumstances. You have the ability to acquire the ability to accept change, to handle uncertainty, and to adapt your plans as necessary. Your capacity for change is an essential quality for accomplishing success in a world that is constantly changing.

How can a student assemble his future?

1. Setting your goals is the first step in putting together your future. In order to construct one's future, one of the most important steps is to create goals.

2. You should regularly engage in self-reflection. It is very important to engage in regular self-reflection in order to gain an awareness of one's personal preferences, strengths, and flaws.

3. Discover your areas of interest. Students should make an effort to investigate their individual passions and interests. Taking part in extracurricular activities, joining clubs, volunteering, or pursuing hobbies are all examples of activities that could fall under this category.

4. Invest in your own academic success. When it comes to planning for the future, excellence is essential.

5. Maintain your motivation.

6. Make yourself more productive by doing things.

7. Master the art of moving on from your past and future.

8. Come forward with a lot of effort to reach your goals in the future, and let go of your negative habits.

9. Continuous skill improvement is absolutely necessary in order to maintain one's relevance in a world that is constantly evolving. It is important to recognize and develop both hard and soft abilities that are in line with your long-term and professional objectives.

10. Establishing a network consisting of peers and mentors is extremely beneficial to your future success. In light of their own experiences, mentors offer direction, counsel, and useful insights to those they are mentoring.

CHAPTER 25

THERE IS NO SHAME IN FAILING

Imagine that you happen to be on a staircase at this same time. A staircase is the means by which one can get to a destination. While you are making your way up the staircase, you have committed an error in the midst of the stairway. What exactly do you do? Do you get up and keep moving forward to the next level? Or do. In this chapter, I will tell you about failure and how you can tackle them.

You have made the decision to take a tumble down the stairs, which will render the progress you have made toward reaching your goal null and void.

Procrastination occurs when an individual is unable to acknowledge the errors that they have made as a result of Procrastination. Experiencing irritation, sadness, rage, guilt, and grief are all possible outcomes that might result from making mistakes. These are all unfavorable and unsettling emotions to experience. While it is reasonable and normal to have these sentiments after making a mistake, dwelling on them for an extended period of time will only make you more prone to suffering from depression. You are putting yourself in a position to suffer and experience unpleasant emotions in order to undermine yourself if you make a mistake and are unable to let it fade away.

Don't forget that you are a human being. Expect to make mistakes and not to avoid them. It is impossible to find a single living person who has never committed an error in their lifetime during their lifetime. When people are young, they are prone to making mistakes, and the only thing they can do is learn from those mistakes while they are still young. It is important to take into consideration the number of cups that toddlers have to spill before they are able to drink from this cup. Although the cups are a complete mess, the toddler would not have been able to drink from a cup if it were not for the mistakes that were made.

Methods for overcoming your past failures.

It sounds simpler than it is in practice. Although accepting forgiveness for oneself becomes easier with time, it can be challenging at first. In order to have a great future, these ways can make it much easier to forget your past mistakes.

Learn to forgive yourself.

To forgive yourself, you must first put your past in the past. No two people's stories are the same, and some are more challenging than others. Focusing on making improvements is the most effective way to forgive yourself if you are grappling with a mistake from your past. If you are sick to your stomach from being mad at yourself, it may help to put the past in the past. Your actions have the power to shape your future, so remember that you always have the choice to do better. When you dwell on your former self all the time, this becomes impossible. Rather, focus on improving yourself to your fullest potential.

It is okay to make mistakes.

Making mistakes is a natural part of learning, and it is perfectly fine to do so. Embracing your shortcomings and errors is crucial since they have the power to greatly influence your judgment. Research shows that people with a lot of knowledge in a certain field are less likely to see mistakes and fix them because they are confident in their own judgment. Being mistake-tolerant increases the likelihood that you will identify and address the problem of Procrastination before it escalates. On top of that, when you let yourself make errors without beating yourself up, you build confidence by challenging yourself.

Make yourself your own best friend.

You can become your own best friend by talking about yourself in the same way that you would talk about your best friend. It is far more difficult to criticize the acts of those that you hold dear despite the fact that we constantly make ourselves feel bad for our own flaws. In situations where someone is overly critical of oneself, it can be beneficial to imagine that you are someone that you hold in high regard. Take into consideration the ways in which you would assist them in overcoming their errors and Procrastination and the guidance that you would offer them. After that, you will be able to provide yourself with the same direction.

Take responsibility for your actions.

Consider taking responsibility for the errors you made in the past. When you are held accountable for the activities that you perform, it is much simpler to make amends for mistakes that you have undertaken. You must first acknowledge that you are responsible for your actions before you can accept that you have failed. In addition to developing a plan of action to improve your habits, you should remind them that you have apologized. Unfortunately, it is not possible to rectify errors that have already been made. On the other hand, you have the ability to modify your patterns of behavior for the subsequent occasion. Acquiring knowledge about your shortcomings can be advantageous, particularly in situations where you have caused offense or injury to yourself.

Identifying the source of your mistakes.

Determine what caused the Procrastination. If you can figure out what went wrong, you might be able to prevent making the same mistake in the future. For illustration's sake, let us say you have become friends with someone. A few weeks in, your trusted friend warns you about the person's lack of reliability. They steal from you because you have faith in your judgment. You are not to blame; rather, the responsibility rests with their collaborators. Even though you wish to avoid danger in the future, remember that you were acting recklessly when you put it off. Based on your current level of awareness, you were behaving responsibly. Investigate the reasons behind your failure due to Procrastination and address them.

Your re-evaluation.

Think about your principles and values again. Consider your most important values if you find it difficult to let go. In what ways do you intend to present yourself? So, how exactly do you plan to act? When you behave in a way that goes against your principles, Maybe it is a chance to reevaluate the decisions you have been making. You may be able to come to terms with your shortcomings if you do this.

Get a "do-over"; you owe it to yourself. The second time around, you have a better chance of getting it right. Obviously, there are times when exactly the same thing can't happen again. Contemplate what happened and write down the things you could have done differently. This shows that you have taken the time to reflect on and apply the lessons from your mistakes. Plus, you're improving your skills for when you have to deal with comparable challenges in the future.

CHAPTER 26

A FUTURE FREE OF PROCRASTINATION: A CHANCE FOR YOU TO SHINE

Omission bias plays a role in students procrastinating. Procrastination is frequently caused by omission bias. To put it simply, procrastination is the tendency to put off completing what we had planned to do. We are less likely to be concerned about our procrastination tendencies because we have a predisposition toward weighing the benefits and drawbacks of doing nothing. Since we aren't actually doing anything, our brains automatically assume that everything is fine.

We ask ourselves, "How can we be in the wrong if we're doing absolutely nothing?" Our mind's "logic" is deceiving; it bends reason to justify delay so we may keep enjoying the short-term benefits while ignoring the long-term costs.

Role of Omission Bias

Why do we persist in putting things off till later when we are aware that it hurts us?

And what about the mental reasons behind our inclination to do something that gets in the way of our plans? What is it about the human mind and brain that makes us prone to procrastinate until later, even when we are aware that we ought to be completing them right this second?

This question can be explained by omission bias. The inability to perceive the repercussions of doing nothing is known as omission bias, a form of cognitive distortion.

The costs of doing nothing are more difficult to fathom than the repercussions of doing something wrong. This is because our brains are hardwired to expect a certain outcome whenever we take part in or see an action. We will observe the subsequent events with interest. Our minds do not bother to try to imagine how something might improve our situation when there is not any real action to take.

self-awareness concerning omission bias

When you are stuck because of omission bias, how do you break free?

Growing self-aware is the first step. You will be more driven to start doing anything once you realize how serious the consequences are if you do not. Learn to identify the signs of omission bias in your academic life, how it has undermined your drive to complete assignments in the past, and how it will influence your choices and behaviors moving forward.

You can win this battle.

You are fighting against yourself, and you have the ability to prevail in this conflict. Believe me when I say that you can prevail in this conflict by yourself. In the event that you are willing to alter the path that your future takes, there is nothing that is impossible for you to do. You will be able to do so. It is beyond any reasonable dispute.

Irresistibly, there are times when we have to force ourselves to carry out actions that we would rather not. In fact, that is one of the most important aspects of practicing and improving anything. We are momentarily duped by the advantage or the ultimate result to the extent that we are able to smile and tolerate the agony that is currently being experienced.

A significant number of us believe that we are only able to work when we are in the mood for it or when we are struck by inspiration. It is a struggle that cannot be won. When it comes to getting where you want to go, you should not rely on your mood. Conversely, you should think in the opposite direction: once you start doing action, your mood will follow suit. It is important to forgive yourself for putting things off in the past since doing so will prevent you from falling into the waves of failure and giving up completely.

Learn to recognize and overcome omission bias. This is the moment when you come to the realization that it is simple to feel the impact of doing something, but it is far more difficult to feel the impact of not doing something. This is about more than just being aware of the situation; you may combat omission bias by actively visualizing the negative future that you are creating for yourself. That will get you gearing up for the race.

Begin to get out of your comfort zone and start the process of initiation right away.

Procrastination is a factor that contributes to difficulties in starting an activity. It is difficult for you to begin doing what you ought to be doing; instead, you continue to participate in other things that you find to be more enjoyable. You arrange a "start time" for each of the chores that you intend to complete, but once that time arrives, you always find an excuse to postpone the start to a different time.

Take the following example into consideration. You have to get yourself ready for the impending examinations. The time is 8:30

in the morning. Supposedly, you will prepare yourself for the hectic day that lies ahead by saying, "I'll start at 9:00 AM," and then on to engage in other pointless and random activities. It is 9:15 in the morning when you get a chance to look at the clock again. "No, I'll begin at ten o'clock in the morning," you decide. You may refer to it as your Perfectionist self just wanting to start things right and correctly, but you are aware of the fact that the real issue is that you simply do not have the motivation to begin. You should, therefore, take an oath with yourself that I will begin working on myself and my better future from this very moment onward. In order to improve your future and your fight against Procrastination, you should take the initiative. Specifically, this refers to your capacity to initiate and get started on activities or tasks without much effort. You are able to break the inertia of inactivity and take the first step toward completing the task at hand, or any task for that matter, because it is what enables you to do so. You will always find that the first step is the most difficult to take, but it will ultimately show you results in the future. Your ability to come up with ideas and solutions for problem-solving on your own is also a component of task initiation. In the event that this function is lacking, you will realize that it is quite challenging to initiate duties and combat your negative behaviors. Get out of your shell and work for a better and bright future.

CONCLUSION

Consider your most recent decision-making experience. Was it to get in touch with Mom?

Maybe skip the local train and get on the express one, or ignore the yellow light and continue? Each of us makes hundreds of these seemingly insignificant decisions daily, and the vast majority of these turn out to be right. Going through the yellow light may have been the best option if you avoided an accident or could have gotten to work faster by using the express. If humans weren't generally good decision-makers, we'd be in constant conflict with one another, unable to function in daily life.

More challenging decisions, such as accepting an offer or deciding whether or not to perform a task, are something that we all have to make. Choosing to combat Procrastination has the power to transform your life.

The ability to combat Procrastination is not something that can be acquired solely via the study of books. Give me a moment to bring you down to earth. If you take this book and keep it in your head at all times, you will never experience any change. This is a possibility. In order for your ideal future to become a reality in your life, you will need to actively seek it out and put in the effort to grow it.

Moreover, you need to be able to put it into action. You should not just sit around and wait for the time to come when everything will be "just perfect" to ensure your future. I cannot wait for you to begin making progress toward a better future for yourself. Due to the possibility that tomorrow will be too late, you need to start today. It is a positive aspect of the situation. that it is simpler than you might think to overcome the habit of Procrastination. How come? The reason for this is that you already have something that you put your faith in.

Every one of us is driven by our own individual interests. Interests are something that everyone possesses. We have the ability to pursue everything we desire if we decide to pursue these interests and ambitions. If you are content with who you are, you will have a stronger belief that you are deserving of success, which will result in a more positive image for you in the future. Once you have achieved this level, you can continue to improve it until you are able to project it as an ability that you possess.

Then, people will immediately believe that you are conscious of the way in which you provide your values to others. If you'd rather concentrate on the positive, by all means do so; just be sure to note anything that can dampen or even halt your delight. Identifying and monitoring your talents and weaknesses is important if you value them.

You must always keep these in mind, regardless of the circumstances.

Always keep in mind that this is the moment when you ought to shine. There is no obstacle that can be overcome by a guy who is unwilling to listen to reason. People will tell you that you are irrational if you set goals that are too ambitious. However, they have described a great number of successful inventors and other individuals who have altered the course of history. Refrain from listening to anyone other than yourself and your own thoughts. Never stop believing. If you want to be successful, you have to have faith in your own capabilities. Make sure you never forget the things that are significant to you on a personal level.

Regarding your self-efficacy, there are three incredibly crucial aspects that you need to be aware of. You can construct it by earning a series of little victories and remaining steadfast in the face of failures. It is possible to boost your self-assurance by modeling your behavior after that of others; your previous achievements will boost your overall self-assurance and assist you in accomplishing additional objectives.

Remember that nobody has ever accomplished significant goals in a short amount of time. You begin with relatively minor accomplishments and gradually work your way up to more significant levels of success. Waiting will only result in inaction and the waste of time, so rather than putting things off, you should start taking action to ensure a good future for yourself.

You should always have faith and ask yourself how you can accomplish your 10-year objective in a period of little more than six months. In many cases, we put off achieving our objectives simply because we are unable to think creatively or because we invent excuses. Taking your time and remaining consistent will ensure that you are able to achieve your objective and live the life of your dreams. There is no doubt about it. Work hard for your dreams, and there is no doubt that you will surely achieve it.

ACKNOWLEDGMENTS

Writing this book has been one of personal development and profound appreciation. This would not have been possible without the help and encouragement of many people and organizations.

First and foremost, I offer my sincere appreciation to my family and friends for their constant support and understanding during this attempt. Your unwavering support and confidence in my abilities have been an endless well of creativity.

I sincerely thank the specialists and industry professionals who generously contributed to this book by sharing their expertise and experience. Your contributions to these pages have increased their depth and reliability.

The publishing company deserves our gratitude for their tireless efforts in bringing this book to fruition. Your skills and commitment to quality have been important in developing our project.

In addition, I'd like to thank the readers whose interest in these issues has encouraged me to learn more about them. This effort has been motivated by your enthusiasm and participation.

Last but not least, I want to express my gratitude to everyone who has helped me along the way, whether or not their names are mentioned in the text.

Thank you again, and be the best Adult you can be!

REFERENCES

1. https://www.everand.com/read/270507096/How-to-Think-Bigger-Aim-Higher-Get-More-Motivated-and-Accomplish-Big-Things

2. https://www.verywellmind.com/the-psychology-of-procrastination-2795944

3. https://www.everand.com/read/457786410/The-Science-of-Overcoming-Procrastination-How-to-Be-Disciplined-Break-Inertia-Manage-Your-Time-and-Be-Productive-Get-Off-Your-Butt-and-Get-Things

4. https://www.everand.com/read/270507096/How-to-Think-Bigger-Aim-Higher-Get-More-Motivated-and-Accomplish-Big-Things

5. https://www.everand.com/read/383551395/How-to-Study-The-Program-That-Has-Helped-Millions-of-Students-Study-Smarter-Not-Harder#__search-menu_744514

6. https://www.everand.com/book/233244185/Procrastination-Motivation-and-You

7. https://www.everand.com/book/467589693/Productivi
    ty-How-to-Be-Ten-Times-More-Productive-With-Your-
    Day-How-Good-Habits-Can-Increase-Your-Productivity

8. https://www.everand.com/read/340242642/Meditation
    -Meditation-for-beginners-Learn-to-build-a-daily-
    meditation-habit-calm-your-mind-increase-happiness-
    success-health-memory-concentrat

9. https://www.everand.com/read/644543816/It-Starts-
    with-Self-Compassion-A-Practical-Road-Map